RIDING SHOTGUN

ACHIEVING THE SHOTGUN WILLIE'S EXPERIENCE

Deborah Matthews Dunafon & Michele Poague

For information contact:
Bent Briar Publishing L.L.L.P.
Denver CO
www.bentbriarbooks.com

ISBNs
978-1-942665-14-4   SC
978-1-942665-15-1   EPUB

First Edition: April 2021

10 9 8 7 6 5 4 3 2 1

TABLE OF CONTENTS

ABOUT THE AUTHORS

Deborah Matthews Dunafon
A current board member and past president of the Glendale Chamber of Commerce, she is the majority owner and CEO of Shotgun Willie's, Denver's iconic gentlemen's' club since 1982. She serves on several other community boards, and non-profit groups including the Dunafon Family Foundation created for helping kids at risk.

Michele Poague
In addition to her 35+ years in multiple roles at Shotgun Willie's, Michele Poague is an accomplished special events planner, a dedicated political activist, and a published author. Her fiction works include the multiple-award-winning trilogy, *The Healing Crystal, The Candy Store, and The Broken Shade.*

DEDICATION

To our good friend and mentor, Dan Griffith: You are missed.

PREFACE

WHAT IS THE SHOTGUN WILLIE'S EXPERIENCE?

The best entertainers in the business and a loyal staff offering *Five-Star Service* combine to create an elegant gentlemen's club atmosphere where patrons can relax and enjoy themselves.

In an industry where adult entertainment clubs come and go, Shotgun Willie's is a rare gem now in its fourth decade of business in Glendale, Colorado. Keys to achieving this level of success include eliminating the hustle, providing a great show, being a viable member of the community, and helping employees. Time-tested policies and procedures combined with superior training and support are at Shotgun Willie's core.

ARE YOU CREATING OR IMPROVING A GENTLEMEN'S CLUB?

This book is a powerful tool that can help you achieve the Shotgun Willie's experience. Ride along to discover how to develop a great show, how to manage the inherent chaos, and how staff members are tasked and trained, including policy and procedure examples and sample forms to help you create or improve your own special club.

WARNING AND DISCLAIMER

Shotgun Willie's and this book are NOT politically correct!
The content and opinions represented in this book are **not** to be considered as legal or accounting advice.

CHAPTER 1 | INTRODUCTION

Although this is a $75 billion industry, it isn't for everyone. Before we get into talking about who we are, let us examine a little history of the industry overall.

We wouldn't be surprised if the first striptease began when a cave-man built a fire and, in his excitement, began to beat on a wooden dish.

Throughout history, most societies celebrated sexuality through various fertility dances and festivals. Of course, back then, it was all about having babies, but that didn't mean it wasn't any fun.

A LITTLE HISTORY

The ancient Roman festival of Lupercalia was celebrated on February fifteenth. Among other strange customs, a priest would run around whipping women with thongs made from a sacrificed goat.

The Celts, unlike the Victorians, weren't shy about sexuality. Beltane is all about sex and fertility and was the second most sacred of Celtic festivals. It was a celebration of the sexual union of the God and Goddess. Maypole dances were an ancient fertility rite in which the pole is a phallic symbol, the ribbons represent its union with the feminine, and the dance represents the act of intercourse.

While we can't know for sure if women danced for men in 500 B.C. we're going to suggest that it happened rather frequently. Evidence of the pagan ritual origin of early Georgian dances can be traced to the second millennium B.C. A bone plate from this period depicts a dancing woman, suggesting a female ritual usually performed during the harvesting season in front of statues of the goddess of fertility. One of the fertility goddesses of the Caucasus was Anahita, who also represented sexuality and love.

The sun goddess Nana was also honored with a dance from the Kartuli-Kakhetian region. The song which accompanied the dance to Nana gradually lost its original meaning after the introduction of Christianity to Georgia in 337 A.D.

Under the rule of Queen Tamar (1184-1213), Georgia experienced its "Golden Age" and became one of the strongest kingdoms in the Near East. It is from here we find the dance of *Kartuli* in which the ritualistic conduct of the male toward his partner is strictly governed by a set of rules. The female leads and the male must follow her path of direction. He must never touch the woman, not even with the fabric of his coat; to do so shows a lack of respect and could be interpreted as an insult. Sound familiar?

Perhaps one of the most famous historic dances is the Dance of the Seven Veils. According to Wikipedia, the Dance of the Seven Veils is an elaboration on the biblical story, which refers to Salome dancing before King Herod. Being struck by her beauty and grace, Herod offers to grant her any wish. She asks for the execution of John the Baptist.

The name *Dance of the Seven Veils* originates with the 1893 English translation from Oscar Wilde's 1891 French play *Salome* in which the title character dances the dance of the seven veils, seductively removing the veils one at a time. Wilde's choice of title for the dance might also be linked to the popularity of the "veil dances" from the Far East during the late nineteenth century and *Folies Bergère* in Paris, which was becoming famous for its a cabaret music featuring beautiful women dancing in revealing and provocative costumes.

While vaudeville and burlesque had its share of pretty dancing girls, it was the circus that brought the Far Eastern style of dance to the masses. This included the provocative "belly dance" or as it was sometimes billed, the *Hoochie Coochie*. While belly dancing can be traced back to ancient Egypt, leave it to the west to exploit the sensuality of a bare belly.

While peep shows often depicted women undressing, it was the Minsky brothers who brought burlesque to the masses and became known as "the poor man's Follies." This burlesque empire was a family business set up by four brothers: Abraham (Abe), Billy, Herbert, and Morton Minsky. The brothers joined forces in 1912 but were eventually closed in 1937 due to censorship. The word *striptease* finds its origin in a review written about one of their New York shows. Gypsy Rose Lee, the godmother of modern-day striptease, began her career with Minsky's Burlesque.

In the 1940's we see the rise of the pinup girl and America is introduced once again to scantily clad women. During this time, while movies began to replace most live entertainment, small theaters with a few women willing to bare their assets gave rise to the strip club.

By the end of the '50s, burlesque-type shows had given way to the "hustle club." During the '60s and '70s, these strip clubs usually had a main stage where a woman would dance nude or partially nude for an all-male audience. When the entertainer finished her dance, she would find a patron to sit with and convince him to buy drinks at ridiculous prices. Quite often, the lady was drinking nothing more than sparkling apple juice or sodas, but the price was more suited to a case of liquor. The house then paid her a commission on the number of drinks she could hustle. Hence the term "hustle club."

In many of these places, a dancer would take the patron into a private room and shake him down. She would take his money and promise a variety of exotic activities only to slip out the back door, or usually into the dressing room until the guy got tired of waiting. In the early '80s, there were larger clubs popping up across the country that had one thing in common: the hustle. A man couldn't hand over a credit card without expecting to pay a month's salary to get it back.

The late '80s brought a revival of burlesque. It all started with a desire to do something better than the typical strip club where a man had to hang on to his wallet when he stepped through the door.

SHOTGUN WILLIE'S - A NEW IDEA

In 1982, Debbie Matthews, working with friends, Dan Griffith and Hal Lowery, developed a new way to do business. Keys to the success of their venture included eliminating the hustle, providing a great show, being a viable member of the community, and helping employees.

Eliminating the Hustle

Shotgun Willie's doesn't charge a different price for an entertainer's drink. They charge a reasonable price at the door, and their drink prices are in line with what you would pay at the airport. (Sadly, the only thing you'll see takin' off there are planes).

One of the major differences between Shotgun Willie's and their competition is that they don't encourage their entertainers to drink. A sloppy, drunk woman isn't attractive, and she's a liability to your liquor license. Any woman that feels she needs to be drunk or high to do this job is in the wrong business.

Providing a Great Show

Dan, being Disney trained, taught Debbie and Hal how important it is to train the staff to think of the entire club as a stage and every employee a part of the show.

Treating employees as valuable cast members of your show creates a team atmosphere and engenders loyalty to the show and to each other. A testament to that is the number of employees who have been with Shotgun Willie's for twenty or more years. Managers are all Disney-trained to be the best kind of show business managers we can have. Shotgun Willie's designed several choreographed dance numbers, the most popular one being the *Rodeo* song. All the entertainers dressed in Daisy Dukes, plaid shirts, and cowboy hats. *Get Down Tonight* was a salute to the '70s with entertainers wearing halter-tops and bellbottom pants. For our nod to the '90s, guests were invited on stage to dance the *Macarena* with their favorite girl. Among other dances, our entertainers also performed *New York, New York* in top hats and tails. When you saw a chorus line of 40 to 50 entertainers doing high kicks, you knew Shotgun Willie's was a step above the rest. During the 80s and 90s, all entertainers were required to learn and perform these choreographed numbers each night.

Instead of one stage, or one large stage, and a couple of small stages like so many of the other clubs, Shotgun Willie's has seven large stages at tabletop height. The stages are black glass, which reflects the beautiful girl and the chandeliers. The barrier between guests and entertainers is a small black pad around the edges of the stage to protect the entertainer's knees when she bends down to take a tip.

Each entertainer dances for three songs and then is on her own to entertain tableside for the next six to nine songs. When called back to the stage, she will dance on a new stage on the other side of the room from her last performance. By the end of the night, each entertainer will have danced on every stage, meaning a guest can sit in one place and see a constant stream of new pretty women. Keep in mind, the more beautiful women you have on stage, the more money the business will make.

Being a Viable Member of the Community
It's not just about making sure our guests have a wonderful time. We also give back to the community.

Since the 1980s, Shotgun Willie's has hosted an annual Charity Golf Tournament. Proceeds go to national charities as well as helping the people who work for us. For over thirty years, Shotgun Willie's and its employees have raised thousands of dollars for The Wounded Warriors Project, Cystic Fibrosis, and Tennyson House for Children at Risk, to name only a few.

Shotgun Willie's also hosts an annual "Feed the Homeless" dinner at which entertainers and employees pitch in money and time to feed over one hundred homeless people every November. We provide blankets, socks, gloves, and a hot meal. Being able to give to those less fortunate is humbling and teaches us to appreciate how lucky we are.

We feel it's important for employees to share in these charity events.
Feeling like you are part of something larger than yourself - something
altruistic - engenders loyalty. It's the loyalty of our employees that keeps
us so far above the other clubs.

Helping Employees

Here are a few of numerous instances where Shotgun Willie's helped its
many employees over the years:

- A former entertainer was paralyzed in a car accident. The Golf
  Tournament proceeds bought an electric wheelchair for her.
- Golf tournament funds also helped a waitress get reconstructive
  surgery after having a mastectomy.

- Another employee's sister lost everything in a fire. Shotgun Willie's raised several thousand dollars for her.
- A bartender was killed in a motorcycle accident leaving behind a six-year-old daughter without insurance. Shotgun Willie's opened a trust fund and continued to pay her father's weekly salary until she was 18.
- When a DJ died of a brain tumor, Shotgun Willie's started a trust fund for his daughter as well.
- An entertainer was addicted to opioids. The club spent $35,000 to put her through an in-house recovery program. She is still with us today.
- We have established an "After Shotguns" scholarship program. We realize, much like the professional athlete, our entertainers will only be able to dance for a limited number of years. We offer these scholarships to those who want to plan for their future. A trapped entertainer is never a happy entertainer.

It doesn't stop there. Every year we find new ways to help people.

That loyalty led to the employee support we had when the city tried to shut us down in the late '90s.

ALL POLITICS ARE LOCAL

Glendale is a 382-acre community dominated by small businesses, strip malls, apartment complexes and condominiums surrounded by south Denver. The city has one single-family home, and the average age is 28. Apartments are relatively cheap, and 85% of the residents are renters, who typically stay less than a year. Although Glendale has about 4,100 residents, its daytime population swells to about 25,000 workers in retail, office complexes, and two telemarketing centers. The two strip joints in town outnumber the lone church. Glendale is the kind of place that most people just pass through.

Joe Rice, elected mayor of this Denver suburb in 1996, wanted to make Glendale more "family-friendly." During the fall of 1997, Mr. Rice came across some literature from a conservative legal group on how to draft a lawsuit-proof strip-club ordinance; in January, he formally proposed a law based on the group's model. Tired of having his city's claim to fame being the world-famous Shotgun Willie's, Mr. Rice partnered with Focus on the Family and the National Family Legal Foundation (NFLF), whose modus operandi was to kill adult businesses with regulations and ordinances. In fact, the NFLF had been successful in closing more than 480 businesses across the country.

The ordinance, known as Ordinance 4, wouldn't ban topless clubs outright. Instead, it would:

- raise the minimum age of dancers from 18 to 21;
- ban so-called table dancing (during which there may be physical contact between performer and patron);
- require that tips go to a central fund rather than being tucked into dancers' G-strings by the patron;
- require the entertainment cease at midnight;
- require lighting changes that had more in common with a retail store than a nightclub or cocktail lounge.

When was the last time you were in any bar or restaurant that was lit brighter than a shopping mall?

In addition to a complete lack of common sense, the majority of claims the NFLF made in their opinion pieces were half-truths and blatant lies. For example, they blatantly lied when they claimed that tipping an entertainer by placing a dollar in her G-String caused the spread of AIDS. We can't think of one instance where a person contracted an STD by handing a girl a dollar. They also falsely claimed adult business increased the number of rapes and sexual assaults and that the local police force was spending all their time handling violent crimes at, or around, these businesses. When asked to testify, the local police chief stated that the business with the highest number of calls was a local discount store.

Some of the other ordinances suggested by the NFLF were truly idiotic, like requiring the entertainment stop at midnight so men could have a two-hour "cooling down period." Did they really think, without entertainment, the guests would wait around for two hours before going home? And what about the guy who stopped in for a beer after work? What were we to do? Lock him in a room for two hours so he could "cool down"?

This was beyond stupid.

At one of the council meetings, Rice went so far as to claim Ordinance 4 should be passed because these hard-working women would be better off on welfare.

The city council fully expected staunch support from residents and business owners. However, the city's young population wasn't impressed by the evocations of family values, and the business establishment in this small town was deeply suspicious of any regulations. So what they got was a full-scale revolt. The city council was surprised to find Shotgun Willie's was accepted, if not well-liked, by the citizens of Glendale.

It wasn't a slam dunk. We had to break out the big guns. This small-town revolt took thousands of dollars and more than a hundred volunteers. We began by looking for money and candidates to run against the mayor's allies on the City Council.

It has been said, in a political war, you must define your enemy before they define you. There was no hiding what we were, so we embraced it. In a tiny office in the basement of Shotgun Willie's, we printed party invitations, flyers, and postcards, all the while, taking turns sleeping on the floor to make sure the printer didn't run out of ink or paper. Each day we would hit the streets with the latest item, hot off the press.

Together with other Glendale business owners, we formed a new political party to oust the mayor's allies from the City Council. We called ourselves the Glendale Tea Party, after an earlier act of economic rebellion. We were being taxed, but our representation did not give a crap about our employees or us. Like our forefathers, we were fighting for freedom, the freedom to have a business that at least a fair portion of the public supported. Our cheer was "Throw Rice in the harbor."

Friendly restaurants and small bars held fundraisers featuring free food and beer. There were powerful speakers at these regular events praising liberty and the rights of the citizen to choose the people who represent them. We handed out copies of Ordinance 4 and asked the citizens of Glendale to save our jobs.

The first step in fighting city hall is to meet the voters. Exotic dancers and local business owners canvassed door-to-door trying to register sympathetic residents, successfully boosting the number of registered voters by nearly 40%. The canvassers handed out copies of the proposed ordinances and invited residents to the next fundraiser, or as we referred to them, our next "Tea Party."

David Dye, a Rice ally on the City Council, recalls scanning public campaign contribution lists and seeing scores of *Glendale Tea Party* supporters who didn't have personal or financial ties to the strip clubs. Campaign contributions flowed in, eventually totaling $22,000 -- an unheard-of sum in Glendale politics.

We hit pay dirt by linking the topless-bar ordinance to other proposals by Mr. Rice that many businesses objected to, including a previously defeated tax on places serving liquor. The city council was going after independent businesses and the small-business owners stuck together.

All the while, the mayor was chewed out on local talk radio. When a talk radio host denounced Mr. Rice and his allies on the City Council as "pawns of the Christian right-wing," the mayor showed up at the station to respond. The host refused to debate with him, and in a barrage of obscenities that went out over the air, ordered the mayor to leave.

The *Glendale Tea Party* put together a slate of three candidates to challenge incumbent council members in the April 7, 1998 elections: Jay Balano, a former Boston policeman who owned a print shop; Chris Perry, a landscaper; and Kay Parker, a nurse.

After months of campaigning, we discovered this fight wasn't about protecting women from an adult business or making a town of rental apartments more family-friendly.

Shotgun Willie's sits on a prime piece of real estate on one of Denver's busiest thoroughfares. In January of 1998, it became known that a developer wanted to purchase the property for a new hotel. When the owners would not sell, the developer asked the city council to put pressure on the club, including an offer to move down the street and replace another strip club. You see, it wasn't about the undress; it was about the address.

In March, the city council passed the mayor's ordinance, 6-0, but the *Glendale Tea Party* was making progress in the court of public opinion. While Mr. Rice was making a law-and-order appeal about curbing prostitution, drugs, and violence, the Glendale Police Department was notably silent on the issue. The town's sole church, Assumption Greek Orthodox, was also absent from the public debate.

The debate took place in front of the city council as well as major and minor newspapers. The real toehold came from radio talk shows. Once people understood what was happening, many joined our fight. Jay Marvin's talk show had daily callers with drastically different views on the subject. There was a right-wing Christian who called in to tell Jay the world would end if we didn't stop people from having sex, among other extreme views. There was a man who wanted all adult businesses to close because he couldn't control himself and spent all his money at the local XXX movie house.

Several of our employees called in to tell Jay why they worked at Shotgun Willie's. Many of these women were college students fearful of ending up hundreds of thousands of dollars in debt because of rising tuition. There were mothers who liked spending the day with their children and only working 20-25 hours a week to provide a good living for their families. Those of us in the business were not surprised when women called in to say they liked being an entertainer. Some listeners claimed they didn't have the body to dance but would if they could.

On April 7, the *Glendale Tea Party* brought its campaign to a boil claiming town leaders were running roughshod over individual and property rights by trying to restrict the clubs and the three *Glendale Tea Party* candidates were swept into office in an election that brought a record 437 newly registered voters to the polls in a city with an average voter turnout of less than 200. It was a shock to a great many people when we won the election. No one honestly believed a strip club could take on city hall and win.

With one of the mayor's supporters switching sides, the council repealed the ordinance on a 4-2 vote. A few days later, Mr. Dye, an ally to Mr. Rice, resigned, providing the new *Glendale Tea Party* with a solid majority.

Glendale and the city council are supportive of our business because we stay involved in the community and local politics. We meet and make friends with the citizens of Glendale, and we keep a good working relationship with the local police force. More on working with your local police in Chapter 9.

CHAPTER 2 | THE SHOW

Exotic dancing is probably the oldest show on earth.

It is well-documented women like to dance, and men like to watch. Remember your Junior high school dances? Boys against the wall as girls danced with each other.

Note the popularity of Turkish belly dancers and Japanese Geishas?

For thousands of years, Sultan's slaves peeled grapes and hand-fed their masters while other beautiful slaves danced in veils.

If you're going to be a slave, you must admit being a dancer was probably a lot better than hauling rocks to build a pyramid.

Fortunately, these men came to their senses and eliminated slavery, but they could not eliminate men's desire to watch a pretty female dance.

OVERVIEW

Today, women who possess the necessary skills and talent can go anywhere in the world and easily make six figures a year by showing a little skin and dancing sensually. This only works because both men and women like entertainment of this fashion.

According to the Urban Dictionary, "show business" is a vernacular term for the business of entertainment. It tends to refer to the agents, managers, production, and distribution companies that are in the business of entertainment; it can also include the artists and performers involved. It applies to all aspects of live 'shows,' from cinema to television to theater to music.

Never forget strip tease is show business.

The Importance of Choosing the Right Entertainers

When hosting meetings for our staff, the managers often dress up in costumes and put on a show of their own to get a message across.

- In *Snow Drift and the Seven Waifs*, we explored the idea of a new and innocent entertainer meeting a series of less than desirable coworkers: Grumpy the grouch, Doc the drug pusher, Sleazy the hooker, Dopey the drug addict, Bashful the girl who never leaves the dressing room, Sneaky the thief, Clumsy the drunk, and the wickedest of them all, the queen of bad apples. At the end of the skit, the manager/prince saves her from the other girls by showing her how to make money and stay away from those who would do her harm.

- In our *The Wizard of Oz* parody, Glenda gives Dorothy (a girl who has never danced before) a pair of magic shoes that will keep her safe. Dorothy follows the yellow brick road and stops in other clubs filled with flying monkeys (guests who molest her and are rude). Along the way she meets several managers, the Lion who paws at her and makes passes, the Tin Man who is heartless and tells her she must put up with the flying monkeys, and the Scarecrow who isn't smart enough to manage himself let alone a club full of flying monkeys. In the end, she meets a wonderful manager: the wizard who sends her home to Shotgun Willie's.

- In *Finding (Nemo) Dremo*, two managers set out to find the perfect entertainer. While visiting a range of strip clubs, the king and his son are accosted by girls who won't speak to them for less than $100, girls who offer them drugs, girls who are too drunk to talk, and girls who swear like truck drivers. In the end, they find the perfect girl and invite her to work at Shotgun Willie's.

From these outlines you can pick up a steady theme: we want only the best and nicest entertainers.

With that in mind, we have had our share of would-be entertainers we didn't hire. Our usual practice when interviewing a prospective entertainer is to sit with them for a few minutes and ask them simple questions, like "Have you ever danced before? How did you find us? And why do you want to be an entertainer?" Once we are satisfied that the prospective entertainer would be a good fit, we go over the rules and lead her to the dressing room to change into her costume. Imagine my surprise when one prospective entertainer turned out to be a man.

One of our favorite bar backs was autistic. Though he was a very hard worker, he loved to buy women's clothing from the in-house costume supplier. He was always proud to show off his latest purchase of bra and G-string, which he usually wore under his regular clothes.

A WELL-PRODUCED SHOW

A Sense of Professionalism
Imagine you just paid $180 dollars a ticket to see a production of Romeo and Juliet. How would you feel if Juliet walked out on her vine-covered balcony and in answer to Romeo's "Where art thou?" she said, "Where the *fuck* do you think I am? I'm standing right here, you idiot." Or something similar. Of course, you can see how this destroys the fantasy and mood of the show.

Everyone knows Superman can't *really* fly, but it is part of the fantasy you're paying to see. Seeing an entertainer slamming a shot, swilling beer from a bottle, chewing gum on stage, burying herself in her cell phone, or wearing dirty and torn clothing is like seeing Juliet scratching her butt and swearing like a truck driver at Romeo. The waitress who puts on her flats while there are still guests in the club is like seeing Juliet in torn blue jeans instead of a satin and lace frock in the final scene.

The challenge is in teaching your entertainers to see the difference for themselves. Everyone wants to look good and feel good. The manager must re-enforce good behavior every day by making sure the staff knows when they look good. Offering rewards for looking exceptional, for wearing a gown, for having hair and nails done professionally, will encourage the behaviors that make both the entertainer and the club money. Introduce those entertainers who look and act professionally to your guests with money or new guests for a great first impression.

PROPER COSTUMING AND MAKE-UP

Make-up is self-confidence applied directly to the face.
Make-up, hair, and costuming make a dramatic difference. Look at the photo below. Need we say more about this issue? You can see how a great hairstyle, full make-up, and a beautiful dress can make an ordinary woman look spectacular.

LIGHTING MATTERS

Cockroaches love the dark
If you have a beautiful facility and beautiful women, don't hide them.
Most adult clubs are extremely dark, *but bad things can happen in dark corners.*

While we don't propose your club be lit up like a ball field, we do suggest there be enough light that your staff and guests feel safe and aren't tripping over the chairs.

LED lighting is great for light shows but terrible on the skin. When using LED lighting, keep a balance with the incandescent lighting, or your staff will look like zombies. A combination of ultraviolet (blacklight), incandescent red, and incandescent white lighting will hide many flaws on the skin, making your entertainers even more beautiful.

Lighting can change the mood of a room. A doctor's office is stark and well-lit, while your favorite restaurant might have low lighting and candles. The idea behind the incandescent lighting is to simulate sexy and romantic candlelight. The lighting should be low but not so low that your guests are stumbling in virtual darkness.

CHOOSING THE RIGHT MUSIC

Rock 'n' roll is here to stay.
Of all the things that affect your show, music is the most powerful. A good DJ can bring the crowd up or take them down in a matter of minutes. He can have them singing and dancing or have them fighting by playing just the right song.

Rock 'n' roll appeals to more people than any other type of music. That doesn't mean there isn't a place in your club for country and blues. Some of the sexiest songs are traditional blues, but your guests would get tired of your club if that is all your DJ played.

Hip-hop and pop music are huge for the nightclub industry, particularly loud, trendy dance clubs. The pounding beat makes everyone want to get up and dance much the same way classic rock songs encourage people to sing along. The difference is in the crowd hip-hop music attracts. If it's too new or too clubby, it will chase out your older, wealthier guests. Younger people want to hear their favorite song, so you have to accommodate the younger crowd because they are the future of your club. Once a hip-hop song has been on the radio long enough to become classic, it's good for your club.

House and techno music should be reserved for pop music dance nightclubs, and even those have moved away from house music. The days of electronic music, raves, and designer drugs like Ecstasy clubs are fading. It is nearly impossible to choreograph a dance to techno music. Think about the show with every song choice.

Rap music hit the club scene in the 1990s. The message is usually angry and aggressive. Although its popularity cannot be denied, mixing rap with alcohol and drugs is a recipe for disaster. Popular nightclubs targeted to the rap crowd are often short-lived with a history of violence.

DESIGNING THE DJ BOOTH

It's important that the DJ has an unobstructed view of the entire room.
Not only can he monitor the effect his music has on the crowd, but he can also see if the entertainers are on stage, and he can see there is a problem guest. Having access to the microphone, he can notify the management staff of a situation quickly.

Most nightclubs spend a fortune on the DJ booth. With the streaming of music, you no longer need dual turntables and huge racks for vinyl albums. Many professional DJs carry their own library on a portable laptop.

You will also need space for your lighting system computer and your dance board. We recommend a space no larger than six feet by six feet. Anything larger, and you will have to chase your entertainers and guests out of the booth.

Place your sound-system controllers and amplifiers in an easily accessible, secure location with adequate power and cooling. Most sound systems need constant monitoring and cleaning. Having these critical systems in the booth with food and drink is asking for trouble.

A lot of clubs are going to computerized DJs. There is a lot to be said for these systems. You have complete control over song choice. There is never any favoritism. And the computer won't sleep with your entertainers.

When you talk about the cost, the automated system wins out over the DJ and his ego every time. What you give up is the interaction with the crowd. These automated systems can't engage a birthday boy or a bachelor party. Automated systems don't know when an entertainer doesn't make it to the stage or when she leaves a stage unattended. And, from his vantage point, the DJ is also an extra set of eyes for added security.

Remember these tips:

Play for the crowd you want not the crowd you have. Play for your guests not for your entertainers. Play what was popular at the time your average guest was twenty.

Your guests want music that will make them feel good. They want something they can sing along with or music that will make them tap their feet. This music will always keep them in your club.

Your club should not be playing top-forty. Top-forty is what a typical twenty year-old entertainer likes to hear.

If you want a mix of business and blue collar with an average age of 35, (the prime earning years) then take 20 years off the top 40 play list.

A lot of "high rollers" are even older guests. Play music that is 30 and 40 years old. Don't focus on the top dance tunes, pop, or hip-hop. Although there are some good remixes of classic songs.

Play a variety of genres. Throw in the occasional blues or country set. Jazz can add a spark to the show but is more difficult to dance to. The key is a variety of genres and beats. Toss in a slow sexy number to "re-set" the crowd.

When the crowd starts to look rough, play more classic rock and country music. When the crowd seems sluggish, play a well-known-sing-along song like *Sweet Caroline, Black Betty, or Don't Stop Believin'*. When the crowd is tense, slow the music down with a popular ballad.

VOLUME

If I can't hear you, I can't make your drink.

Don't go crazy buying the biggest, most badass speakers. Guests are here to see the entertainer's rack, not your speaker rack.

Keep in mind a lot of your guests want to talk to the entertainers, so the volume needs to be lower over the dining and bottle service seating. If a guest can't hear when an entertainer asks him if he would like a private dance, she won't make money, and he won't have fun. Likewise, if the bartender can't hear the cocktail waitress, drinks will be made wrong, unnecessarily costing the club money.

By evenly spacing your speakers in the ceiling over the stages, you can raise the volume for the dancers and the guests sitting stage-side while keeping the volume slightly lower over the bars and seating areas. At the stage, you want more volume and a heightened sense of excitement. By locating your bass speakers under the stages, it will give both the guest and the entertainer that extra boost they're looking for.

Place smaller speakers over the private dance area and adjust them to a slightly lower level than the stages because the area should be more intimate but still loud enough to make the entertainer want to dance.

SPECIALTY SETS

Never forget your guests are here to see a show.
Sometimes you'll have a talented entertainer who draws a crowd to her stage, but most of the time, you will have a dozen girls of average talent. This is when you can step in and teach your entertainers a simple, but crowd-pleasing, specialty set. It can be as basic as having all the entertainers and staff jump up on a stage or bar for one song to as complex as a fully choreographed number with costuming.

The idea is to break up the rotation often enough to keep the excitement in the room. During those slower afternoons, give your guests something to engage in, like *Dollar Dances* or a *Congo Line*. Playing games like *Butt Bingo, Let's Make a Deal,* or *Putt-Putt Golf* will keep your crowd interested and will cause them to interact with the entertainers. They may be shy at first, but this is why they came in.

We hired feature dancers back in the late 1980s but discovered most guests who came to see the feature left immediately after. They were not spending money on drinks or our entertainers because they were only there for the show.

When we feature our entertainers, the guests stay longer because she stays most of the night, mingling with the guests who came to see her. Another big plus is not raising the cover charge to pay her fees and expenses, all of which was much more than we were bringing in.

We now encourage our entertainers to be featured. They choose their theme, and we outfit them with props, costuming, choreography, and music. Some entertainers need a lot of help, while others need almost nothing.

The concept is to have a catchy three-song feature that guests will remember. Our ideas included *A Salute to the Pin-Up girl, Teacher Teacher, Back to Roaring 20s - Nod to Prohibition,* and *Brooke's Garage.* After a year of these monthly features - many of them quite stunning - we want to see them all again, so every Halloween we hold our *Feature of the Year* contest. Grand prize: $1,000.

CHAPTER 3 | YOUR AUDIENCE

One of the greatest compliments we've ever had might be having a couple of guys bring their dead friend to the club for one last hurrah.

In August of 2011, Jeffrey Jarrett bought his roommate and a friend a round of drinks, Mexican food, and a trip to strip club Shotgun Willie's. While Jarrett was technically present, he wasn't alive to enjoy any of the fun.

When Robert and Mark discovered their friend Jeffrey Jarrett dead, they loaded him into the back seat of Mark's Lincoln Navigator and took him out for the night. The first stop for the trio was the restaurant where Jeffrey had worked, and the last stop was Shotgun Willie's. Jeffrey's body remained in the backseat while his friends drank on his tab. Around 4 a.m., authorities say the pair flagged down a Glendale police officer and told him that Jarrett might be dead.

The two men were charged with abusing a corpse, identity theft, and criminal impersonation, but neither Robert nor Mark were charged with Jarrett's death. Police claim this was about using Jarrett's identity or stealing money, but if that were the motive, why would Mark and Robert have taken the time to load Jeffrey into the car with them.

We choose to believe this was more about saying goodbye to a good friend.

A PLACE WHERE MEN CAN BE MEN

By their nature, strip clubs are not politically correct.
A gentleman's club should be a place where a man can be a man. It's one of the very few places where a man can puff on a cigar and tell a woman he thinks she is beautiful, even sexy, without fear of being sued or losing his job.

In today's corporate America, a man must guard himself against the slightest word or action that might be construed as an unwanted sexual advance. No longer can a man ask a female coworker to have a drink after work, even if his thoughts are totally platonic. Men are visual creatures, but if a female coworker comes in with a new haircut or new dress, a man risks his career if he says it looks nice. It isn't only men who find the female form attractive. Women look at each other all the time. They think nothing of telling a male coworker that Sally's new dress is pretty, but the male coworker dare not comment back.

The sad part of this shift in our culture is the loss of the casual compliment that so often builds confidence and brightens someone's day. Everyone likes to feel good about his or her talents or the way they look. Unfortunately, American society has decided compliments given to the opposite sex are a form of harassment.

Single men and women are finding fewer places to meet potential mates, as is evident by the dramatic rise in dating sites. While some people are willing to meet a potential mate in a bar or nightclub, many don't like the idea of dating someone who hangs out in bars. Even in the bar scene, the potential of being accused of date rape is exceedingly high.

Of course, we don't let men grab or assault our entertainers or staff, but we recognize the entertainment is sensual in nature. We welcome the man who appreciates a pretty woman. We invite men of all levels of society to enjoy a cigar, a fat steak, and the art of the striptease.

TYPES OF CLIENTELE

If a guest has an enjoyable time, he tells his friends, if he has an unpleasant experience, he tells everyone.

Let's begin by looking at several types of bar and nightclub clientele. We've all been to a college bar where the entertainment is usually top forty music and beer pong. How about the country bar with the saw-dusted floor and line dancing? Some people like a local bar where they can hang out with friends and where they know the staff. There are high-energy hip-hop clubs, sports bars, and golf and country clubs. These bars specialize in trendy music and lighting.

Which of the basic demographics do you want to draw from: college students, twenty-somethings, blue-collar workers, white-collar professionals, or major and minor celebrities?

That's a trick question. You want to draw from them all.

Let's look closer at individual guests and see how your format will attract each type of person. We've already established that men of all types and ages like to watch women dance. Even women enjoy watching a pretty female dance if she is really dancing and not just bumping and grinding.

Let's start with those in the 21-29 age bracket:

College Student
- He goes out several times a week.
- He likes to see what's trendy and hip, but most students don't have a lot of disposable income.
- He is often looking for a deal on cover and drinks.
- He likes singles bars where he can "hook-up" with new people.

One night a week that caters to this group will introduce them to your venue. Remember the music you play that night can be age-appropriate and trendier (such as rap or hip-hop) but don't play so much of it that you alienate the rest of your crowd. A new guest can stop in at any time. If "gangsta" rap and hip-hop are blaring from the speakers and this new guest sees what he perceives is a room full of "gangsters," he could tell his friends and business associates that your club was awful at best and scary at worst.

Blue Collar Worker
- This person is who we refer to as *"Joe Six-Pack."*
- He is easy to overlook because he is quiet and steady.
- He is the bread and butter of your club.
- He often enjoys live music or good entertainment more than the pounding club music.
- He will wait in line and pay for the entertainers' drinks so long as the drinks aren't overpriced, and the show is good.

Young Professional
- He will have the most disposable income and the least amount of bills.
- He will most likely be single, without children, and has not purchased a home.
- He will like popular music and will often bounce from place to place.
- He loves to flaunt his money by enjoying tableside and bottle service.
- He doesn't want to wait in lines or pay cover.
- He is showy but usually not a big tipper.

Let's next look at the 30-45 age bracket:

Young Professional
- He is waiting longer to get married but may buy his first home before marriage.
- He will have more disposable income than his younger counterpart but is often more reserved.
- He probably enjoys watching Monday Night Football and drinking beer as much as he likes sushi and a martini.
- He will enjoy a variety of music so long as he can still hold a conversation.
- He will go to clubs to network with other professionals.
- He will usually gravitate to booths and quieter seating areas.
- He tips well but isn't likely to over tip.
- Excellent service is more important to him than his younger counterparts.
- He has been around the block a few times and knows what excellent service is.
- He's looking for the WOW factor.

Working Class
- He is usually more laidback.
- He probably has a wife and children at home.
- He will stop for a drink or two and to meet up with friends.
- He likes to frequent a neighborhood bar. It's about creating relationships.
- He is loyal and likely to be your best regular guest.
- He doesn't usually stay out until the bars close.
- He is more cost-conscious than a professional because he doesn't have as much disposable income.

The 45 and older guest

He still likes to look at pretty girls; however, by this time in his life, the club scene is a memory: sometimes good, sometimes bad.
- His preference leans toward sports bars or jazz clubs if he goes out at all.
- He generally has a more considerable income and is more cost-conscious than a younger person.
- He is often the owner or supervisor of a business.
- He might bring his staff to your club for an afternoon office party but will rarely come in late at night unless he is entertaining clients.
- His music choice will lean toward something familiar and not so loud that conversation is difficult.

Additional Groups

A-Listers, Trust Fund Babies and Club Kids
- This group often comes across as "entitled."
- Don't let your staff get so enamored with these demanding types that your regular guests get ignored.

Actors, Athletes, and Musicians
- These people are fantastic for your business and will spend lots of money.
- It's great advertising for a guest to tell his friends that he met some superstar at your club.
- The professional athlete makes millions and doesn't mind paying for his drinks. But always offer him special seating and special attention.
- Many of these guests like to be discrete when they patronize an adult club.

Groupies

- It's not the professionals that create angst. It's usually their friends and groupies that cause problems. Groupies can be obnoxious and demand VIP treatment, including free drinks and free cover.
- These acquaintances and groupies will develop relationships with your staff. They will begin to expect free drinks and VIP service even when they aren't with the celebrity. Once you have started down this road, it is nearly impossible to reverse the trend.

YOU HAVE A GOOD CROWD, NOW WHAT?

Learn from the mistakes of others; you won't live long enough to make them all yourself.

The single most important function managers perform each shift is to personally meet as many as guests as possible. Most managers resist this function. It might be fear of rejection, inherent shyness, or, more commonly, a misunderstanding of priorities.

Before managers can expect the bar staff and valet to meet and greet guests, they must first set the example.

Successful managers will overcome their fear or shyness and get those priorities in line and will shake hands with as many people as they can during their shift. Many people like to know the managers of the places they frequent. It makes them feel important and cared for. This doesn't happen very often in our business, but it is good sound business practice.

In addition to the fact that meeting guests makes them feel good, there are many other positive results gained from taking the time to talk to your guests. Meeting new people builds confidence and poise, and the staff sees this. In turn, the staff will be more confident in themselves. The communication skills of your staff will grow, resulting in more tips. Seeing positive, friendly managers on the floor gives the entertainers a sense of security and a feeling that the managers have their best interest at heart.

Possibly the best reason for meeting and speaking with guests is the chance to survey them about how they are enjoying the show and the service. Guests will usually speak their mind.

Try questions like *"How is the service? Are you enjoying the music? How is the quality of the entertainment staff? Have any entertainers spoken with you yet? Have you seen our advertisement for the VIP Party? Or other promotion."*

We don't expect you to ask a guest all these questions. These are merely examples of conversation starters that can result in useful information.

KNOWLEDGE IS POWER

The more you know about how your guests perceive your show, the more you can improve their experience.
If several guests tell you the music is too loud or annoying, you have the power to change it. If the service is too slow, you have the power to change it. If they don't know about any upcoming events, you are in a perfect position to inform them.

Adult clubs have a myriad of policies when it comes to tipping and table dances. New guests will welcome the information so as not to make fools of themselves in front of the staff and entertainers.

If a guest mentions a specific entertainer, take the time to escort her to the table for an introduction. The entertainer will never forget this, especially if the guest tips her or buys a dance.

Lastly, when you get to know your guests, you learn about their business and hobbies. If Joe X is into golf and across the room, you have Tom Z, who also plays golf, introduce them to each other. The next time Joe or Tom come into your club, they not only know you, but they have a buddy to drink with. Do this often enough, and you will have dozens of regular guests who become loyal because they feel at home.

Never forget that you are an example to your staff. Teach them how to introduce guests to each other and see their tips soar.

THE JOE SIX-PACK IS YOUR BREAD & BUTTER

Think of your regular guests, the guys who have one or two beers a couple of times a week, as shills.
Not only are the loyal guests the ones who keep the lights on, but they're also the party starters. When new guests come through the door, they don't know anyone. By the time they leave, they should know everyone. It's a lot more fun to drink with other people or share the entertainment experience with a friend. The next time they're looking for a place to have a quick beer, they'll choose to have that beer with friends at your club.

Let's Look at the Math

Four guests buying one $8.50 beer, five days a week
= $170 a week, 52 weeks a year = $8840.
-vs.-
Three guests, buying three $8.50 beers, twice a week
= $153 a week, 52 weeks a year = $7956.
-vs.-
Two guests, buying one $300 bottle, once a month
= $600 a month, 12 months a year = $7200.
-vs.-
One high roller, buying five $300 bottles,
= $1500, four times a year = $6000.

The guest who isn't pressured into spending money he can't afford will be back repeatedly. The guy who isn't insulted for not buying a dance every hour will relax, have fun, and probably spend every dime in his pocket. We have all experienced "Buyer's Remorse." Remember how you felt the next day? You tell yourself you will never put yourself in that position again. If you want to be in business next year, don't let your staff or entertainers ruin the long game.

When a guest feels like the staff talks to him because he's a real person, not a dollar bill, he will open his wallet and feel good about the money he spends. Then he'll be back again on payday. When the high roller does come in, he will see all these people having fun, sharing drinks and stories. Everyone wants to be a part of something exciting. Everyone wants to play with the cool kids. Even the high roller will stay longer and spend more money if he doesn't have to guard his wallet.

OUR MISSION SAYS IT ALL

It is our goal at Shotgun Willie's to create the finest in adult entertainment on the planet.

We do this by treating every person who comes through our doors, calls on our phone, or works with us as a special individual.

We recognize this "spark" of individuality in ourselves as well as in others and communicate this in an honest and sincere manner.

CHAPTER 4 | YOUR ENTERTAINERS

You can have the best service, the best building, and the best drinks, but if you don't have the best entertainment, you have nothing. The name of the game is "pretty girls."

There are many stories about the education level of an exotic dancer. We find the average dancer has two-plus years of college.

In fact, it gave me great pleasure to explain to guests the girl doing pole tricks on stage five was a genuine rocket scientist. She made as much money on a Friday night at Shotgun Willie's as she made as an engineer at Martin Marietta all week.

We have entertainers who have gone on to become police officers, engineers, business owners, and some who saved their money and retired at forty.

Not all of our entertainers are brainiacs. When asked if she knew how to spell Mississippi, one of our entertainers responded with, "The state or the river?" This same young lady was seen rubbing Aspercreme with lidocaine on her forehead because she had a headache.

POPCORN AND MOVIE THEATERS

When you want to see a movie, do you go to a theater that has great popcorn but not the movie you want to see?
Would you base your decision to go to a play on the price of the sodas? Your first criteria will always be the movie or show that's playing. In this business, you must have the movie everyone wants to see. You must have the greatest show on earth.

The Barbara Streisand Syndrome

Many producers and directors hated working with the demanding, bratty, temper tantrum throwing Barbara Streisand, but the box office LOVED her, so she was cast repeatedly, and the directors sucked it up. You will have stars who bring in the crowds, and they might not be the easiest to work with. Your challenge will be in keeping them from storming off and taking their regulars with them. Your club should be the one with the greenest grass. We will spend several chapters showing you how to make your club the one to work for.

The Bad Apple

You have probably heard the expression, "One bad apple can spoil the whole bunch." It has never been truer than in our business when we talk about the support staff and, most especially, the entertainers.

You may, at times, have one or more entertainers with a bad attitude toward other entertainers. Very often, these bad apples run the club in very subtle ways. These clever types are usually friendly with management and a little bossy. They believe they own certain guests (usually high rollers) or certain shifts and use intimidation to control others. New entertainers are a threat to them, and they are skillful and clever at running them off. Their theory is always the same: the fewer the girls, the more money for me.

This is totally wrong. In fact, in our business, it is just the opposite. The more beautiful entertainers and waitresses you have in the club, the more guests you will have and the more money for everyone. There is always more than enough money for the entertainer with the right training and the right attitude. However, the Bad Apple feels the industry owes her everything. She is a taker, not a giver.

The manager must be able to discern this type of person as soon as possible because a rotten apple will ruin the entire staff. They will chase away new and old entertainers. Even your guests will get tired of her hustle and her games and move on to a different club.

This is a genuine problem, and these entertainers or staff members must be identified and dealt with. Be aware: males can be bad apples, too.

Most importantly, a manager must talk to and listen to all the entertainers daily to uncover this kind of situation. Some things to look and listen for are:

- An unusually large turnover of entertainers or staff.
- Staff or entertainers who are bossy, are constantly giving suggestions, and complaining about new girls breaking the rules or not completing their side work.
- Staff or entertainers who gossip about "Club Business" to guests.
- Staff or entertainers who bad mouth other employees or the management team and create cliques.
- Hearing possessive statements like "He's mine. He's my regular. Hands off."
- Refusing to transfer tabs.
- Physical altercations with coworkers, fighting, and swearing in the locker room.

A Bad Apple wants everyone to know she's tough and to fear her. She usually gets cozy with management and threatens to get others fired or have shifts taken away. She is usually on time and dependable because she knows that is the best way to get what she wants from management.

As we said before, as a manager, it is necessary to talk with each entertainer and staff member EVERY DAY to develop a good rapport. This will help you identify the Bad Apples before they can become ingratiated.

Once you have discovered a Bad Apple, you must get rid of them IMMEDIATELY. Make a big deal out of it in front of the entire club. Let it be known that you will not tolerate "bitches" in your club.

You might think ALL people have some of these qualities, and you're right. You must ask yourself how many of these qualities in one person you will tolerate. How much negative impact do certain people have on the club? When are you dealing with Barbara Streisand, and when are you catering to Lizzy Borden?

Mitigating the damage caused by a bad apple
Try to call the entertainers who left recently and let them know the Bad Apple is gone and never should have been hired/contracted in the first place. Ask these staff members and entertainers to stop by so you can talk to them about returning. Start a rebuilding process by creating an atmosphere of unity. This can be achieved by engaging current entertainers in the audition process. Ask their opinion of new girls; ask them to show a new girl around the club and through the locker room; ask them to answer some of the auditions more personal questions. You can even suggest the current entertainer tip the audition if they like her. This makes a new entertainer feel welcome, and she will, in turn, welcome others. Let each person know how important he/she is to the success of the club. Give honest, heartfelt compliments every day.

A STRIPPER VS. AN ENTERTAINER

A picture is worth 1,000 words.
Look at the picture of the women before and after their hair and make-up was done. (See Chapter 2, The Show). Pay attention to the dresses these women are wearing. A professional entertainer will spend the money and time to look her best every time. She will keep her wardrobe and body in shape. Her nails and hair will be professionally done. She understands that by investing in her appearance, she will make her money back tenfold. A professional entertainer understands the essence of female power. She might be going to school to become a helicopter pilot, she might own several rental properties, she might be a concert harpist, and yes, she might be a rocket scientist. We have had the pleasure of working with all these entertainers and many more.

STRIPPERS GIVE STRIP CLUBS A BAD NAME

A stripper will show up in a bra and booty shorts and call it a costume.
Her heels will be worn, and her hair, if styled at all, will be in a simple ponytail or often straight. Her nails will be ragged and chipped if she wears polish. She is often desperate for money. If she's "making bank" it is likely she is hustling your guests, selling drugs, or hooking.

As you walk by the private dance area, you will see the heads of these entertainers popping up like prairie dogs, checking to see if the management has caught them bending the rules.

You will also have transient girls who might be thieves or scammers. These girls move from club to club and are loyal to no one. They are there to make a quick buck any way they can. They will break your rules, making it harder for your loyal entertainers to make money. They will steal from your guest by overcharging or taking money, promising to meet a guest at a hotel, and then not show up. Oddly enough, many of these scammed men will call the next day, expecting to get their money back. Unfortunately, you don't have their money. You can't always make things right, but you can get rid of the girl who is giving your club a bad name.

APPRECIATE THE PEOPLE WHO WORK FOR YOU

You make money when your entertainers make money.
Don't bleed your entertainers dry by requiring them to give their hard-earned money to everyone else. If she's successful, you will be successful. If she's successful, your staff will make lots of tip money from the guests she brings in.

Make your house fees reasonable. Undercutting your competition's fees will only bring in the wrong type of entertainer. Instead, make your club worth the price. Run your own business and never underestimate the value of being a clean, safe, and friendly place to work.

As a caring operator, you must realize this is the kind of business that attracts the worst of society. Often the good entertainer will fall prey to alcohol or drugs. A girl who is used to making $500 to $1,000 a night might believe the money train will never end. In ten years, she's looking old and having trouble making her rent. We feel a responsibility to these women who have provided us with a good living. We understand there are those employees and entertainers who make poor choices. It isn't unusual for us to pay for an employee or entertainer's counseling or rehabilitation.

The best thing you can do for your staff is to teach them how to survive when they leave you. Our training includes money management, safety, and self-esteem. We take the time to teach the staff how to improve their tips by giving exceptional service or value. We teach sales skills that translate to other jobs.

We are always looking to promote from within. This includes promoting entertainers and waitresses to management. We try to introduce our staff to investment or education opportunities, helping them form an exit strategy. Like professional athletes, entertainers can only make a living in this profession for a limited time. Shotgun Willies proudly offers a scholarship program called Willie's Wishes to help transition to life after dancing. Entertainers who are currently enrolled in any vocational school or college program can submit a simple essay to apply for financial assistance.

EMPLOYEE VS. CONTRACTOR

We could author an entire book on the pros and cons of having contract entertainers vs. employees.

To put it simply, if they are your employees you can produce a better show. Unfortunately, many of these girls don't like to be told what to do, and they are quick to go to another venue where they can do as they please.

The IRS requires employers to disclose all income, including tips for every employee. Tracking the cash tips of bar staff and entertainers can be a challenge. The employer must also match social security taxes on these monies. Plan to have triple the accounting and human resources staff to accommodate the added tracking needed for having entertainers as employees.

Having the best show in town will greatly increase your gross sales. Having a venue A-listers and celebrities frequent will put more dollars in your pocket. Having a well-trained staff that performs with little supervision will save training and management dollars. Only you can know if the extra revenue will cover the costs of having entertainers as employees.

A CASE STUDY IN LITIGATION

A Real Eye Opener.
Running any business is more difficult every day, as witnessed by the number of lawsuits filed for everything from changing an employee's hours to advertising the fact that the women who dance in your club are pretty.

Following is a clip from a lawsuit to show how easy it is for an employee to sue without cause. This started when we eliminated a program where we had a concierge who was a waitress, who danced topless for Locker Members. This concierge had been fired the summer before for fighting with coworkers. Because she was a good waitress, we brought her back on the condition she would improve her attitude toward others. No good deed goes unpunished.

Once she returned to work, she began arguing with and complaining about another concierge. Filling the concierge position had become a struggle as our regular waitress staff didn't want to be a concierge, preferring to work as full-time waitresses. When we continued to have problems with this position, we eliminated it and offered the plaintiff a position on the waitress staff. She became belligerent, refused to wear the waitress uniform, and continued fighting with other staff members. We fired her once more because she was far more trouble than she was worth.

Although most of the following charges were proven to be bald-faced lies, and the courts eventually decided in our favor, this case cost the club more than two-hundred thousand dollars to defend.

88.   Plaintiff had numerous guests who wrote letters to owners about her termination stating they made a bad decision about terminating her.

89.   Plaintiff was never talked to about any guest ever complaining about her.

90.   Plaintiff contacted Defendant about obtaining a job and returning to work.

91.   Defendant had previously stated that it wanted Plaintiff to return.

92.   After Plaintiff made her request, Defendant's attorney transmitted correspondence refusing to rehire Plaintiff.

93.   Plaintiff has attempted to mitigate her damages.

94.   Plaintiff notes that Defendant's recent advertising is dispositive as to its sentiments and disrespectfulness toward women in general.

V.   CLAIM FOR RELIEF AND SUPPORTING FACTUAL ALLEGATIONS

Retaliation Premised Upon Gender Based Harassment Complaints

95.   Plaintiff incorporates by reference the preceding allegations.

96.   Plaintiff is member of a protected class, female.

97.   Plaintiff exercised her right to and repeatedly complained about sex-based mistreatment.

98.   Subsequent to her complaints, Defendant took adverse actions against Plaintiff.

99.   Plaintiff was retaliated against by more than one level of management and fired.

100.   Prior to and subsequent to her firing, Plaintiff was the subject of unprotected and concerted activity to harm her by and through the creation of a false police report.

101.   Plaintiff was advised the Defendant wanted Plaintiff to return to work.

102.   Months later when she attempted to return to work, Defendant's attorney in behalf of Defendant, further retaliated by stating Plaintiff would not be rehired.

103.   Defendant itself refused to respond to Plaintiff's rehiring inquiry.

104.   Were it not for Plaintiff's protected activity either the adverse action would not have been taken or the adverse action was a motivating factor in retaliating against Plaintiff.

105.   Defendant intended to and did damage Plaintiff, causing severe emotional distress, mental anguish, loss of enjoyment of life, embarrassment and like hedonic and financial damages.

VI.   DAMAGES

106.   Plaintiff seeks all available remedies authorized by Title VII and the inherent discretionary, equitable authority of this Court including but not limited to:

Back pay;

Front pay;

Compensatory damages;

Punitive damages;

Restorative relief, i.e. a return to work order;

Attorneys' fees;

Costs; and

Interest, prejudgment, post judgment, prejudgment on post judgment.

Our response to the allegations:

89   One letter was written to us, not numerous.

89   We talked to the plaintiff several times and fired her once before for being a "bitch" to others.

90   Plaintiff did contact us, and we said we would not rehire her.

91   We never said we wanted the plaintiff to return after the second time she was fired.

92   Yes, we had our lawyer tell the plaintiff she was not going to be rehired because she refused to take our word.

93   We believe the plaintiff's request to return to work was disingenuous.

94   Our business has always been about sexy women advertising. Our approach hasn't changed in 35 years.

95   If only the preceding allegations were true, which they were not.

96   In the plaintiff's first attempted suit, she claimed age discrimination, although she was hired at age 42 and fired at age 42. We admit she is a female.

97   Never mentioned ANY type of harassment to any manager until after the plaintiff was fired, and we were served with the lawsuit.

98   Because #97 is false, this is false.

99   Because #97 is false, this is false.

100   False. The other waitress-concierge was not coerced into making any statements to anyone.

101   Again, we did not ask the plaintiff to come back to work after the second firing.

102   Yes, as stated before, we had our lawyer send the plaintiff a letter stating the plaintiff would not be rehired because the plaintiff refused to take our word.

103   We responded through our lawyers.

104   There was no retaliation at any time before or after the plaintiff's termination of employment.

105   Although we won in the end, we fought this frivolous case from June of 2015 until December of 2019. We would suggest the plaintiff is guilty of this statement, and it is we who have suffered emotional distress, mental anguish, loss of enjoyment of life, embarrassment, and financial damage.

In her estimate, she lost several hundred thousand dollars in wages alone. Since she lied several times throughout the document, including claiming she was rehired and fired for a third time in 2017 to rescind the statute of limitations, we should seek the above-mentioned damages. (We decided it wasn't worth going after her).

After reading about one of our lawsuits, you may want nothing but contract Entertainers. **BEWARE:** *There are numerous suits around the country where clubs are fined millions because they treat their contract entertainers like employees.* **YOU CAN'T HAVE IT BOTH WAYS.**

The most important thing to remember about using a lease contract for entertainers is that your management team must follow the contract to the letter. This won't guarantee you won't be sued, but it gives your lawyers a fighting chance.

Our contract allows an entertainer to make the choice of being an employee or a contracted lessee. We also renew the contract each year to give the entertainer the opportunity to change her mind or reaffirm her desire to be a contracted lessee.

Our contract has three sections. Part one is the explanation of employee vs. lessee in simple terms. Here an informed choice is made to be either a lessee or employee. The pros and cons of each choice are fully disclosed. Part two is the lessee contract, used only <u>IF</u> that was her choice. If she chooses to be an employee, she must complete the employment package, including the I-9 and W-4. See the chapter on hiring employees. Part three of the contract states the entertainer was offered a copy of her contract, including a list of state laws she must follow, safety rules, and lease fees.

Although we may answer simple questions about things like "what is the employee wage," we NEVER offer legal advice or try to define the meanings of any terms listed in the lessee contract. Since a large majority of the entertainers who audition for us have two-plus years of college, they often have a better understanding of the contract than our managers.

Always give the entertainer time to read the entire contract and the ability to take it to her lawyer or another valued friend for advice. Never, ever sign a contract with an entertainer who has been drinking. Always be sure there is more than one person present when the contract is signed and notarized. The best proof is to have the event filmed. Save these clips, and your lawyer will thank you.

All parts of the contract should be signed, dated, and notarized by both parties. A contract isn't valid if it is not signed by everyone.

CHAPTER 5 | FIVE STAR SERVICE

Your goal should be to create a lasting, memorable, and very positive experience for your guests where the service is so genuine, eager, and consistent that it visibly turns guests into nicer human beings.

To succeed, you need to manage your guests' experiences to not only meet but exceed their expectations.

Your team must strive for professionalism at all times.

WHAT IS FIVE STAR SERVICE?

Five Star Service declares: "Good is not good enough. Only excellence will do."
Keep in mind that not any single point is more important than another; it
is the combination that produces Five Star Service.

To reach your goal, follow these guidelines:

ATTITUDE AND APPEARANCE

*Attitude and appearance go together. If you look good, you feel
good, and if you feel good, you look good. If you act like you're
having fun, those around you will have fun.*

There is no room on the floor for personal problems.
Not only does it affect your performance, but it also affects those around
you. Our guests come here to see beautiful women and have an enjoyable
time. They notice little things like hair and fingernails. It is difficult to be
"perfect" every day but expect your staff to do the very best they can.

Have uniforms or a dress code for your staff. You want the guest to be
able to identify who is working. Set a standard of dress because your
guests deserve the best in show business. The costume/uniform is part of
the show.

A healthy staff will look good and have more energy. Drugs have no place
in your club and can only lead to poor health. Excessive drinking will
damage the skin as well as the liver. Keep in mind that language is as
much a part of the appearance as the uniform.

Most clubs are very dark, and the red lights wash out blemishes as well as
the colors in the face. Your entire staff is on stage and should wear stage
make-up.

KNOWLEDGE

Your staff should know their duties and responsibilities thoroughly. They should know all procedures and promotions. If there is something they don't know or understand, they should ASK.

The worst thing you can say to a guest is, "I don't know." This response suggests you don't care. It is far better to say: "I'll find out," or "I'll check on that for you."

Imagine trying to sell insurance if you don't know what aggregate, deferred annuity, or indemnity means. Could you sell houses without an understanding of escrow, appraisal, and equity? Your staff can't sell alcohol if they don't know anything about alcohol. For example:

- Do they know the seven different names for *Khalúa and Cream*?
- Do they know what a *High-Ball* is?
- How about a *7-High*?
- What would they serve if someone asked for a *Bourbon Ditch*?
- What does the term *Neat* mean?
- What is the difference between *Jack Daniels* and *Crown Royal*?
- What replacement would they offer the guest who asks for *Black Velvet*? *Bullet*? *Cazadores*?

Take the time to continually train your staff. Take advantage of liquor company sales representative training, but be aware, when it comes to the latest fad drink, wait until you have had dozens of requests before adding it to inventory. Most people won't try something new at the prices we charge, no matter how hard the bartender pushes it.

It also helps your staff if you don't continuously change your inventory. Remember, your guests come to see the girls. If you don't have Jim Beam, they will probably drink Jack Daniels.

SERVICE

Service is the art of making the guest feel as if he is the only person in the room. Your staff must cater to the guests. They must do the extra little things to make every guest feel special.

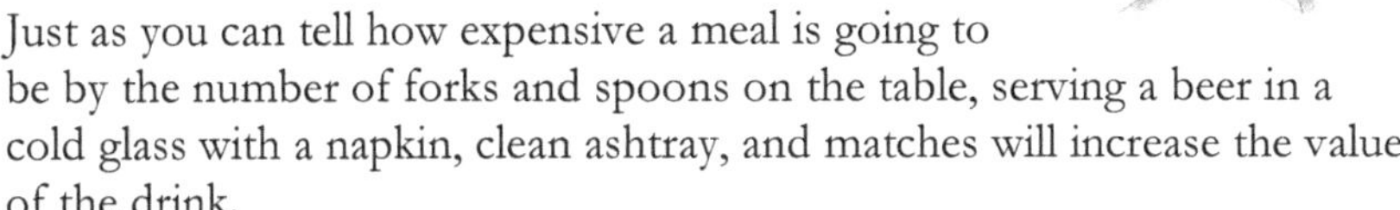

Just as you can tell how expensive a meal is going to be by the number of forks and spoons on the table, serving a beer in a cold glass with a napkin, clean ashtray, and matches will increase the value of the drink.

Offering a food menu will enhance the experience even if the guest doesn't order. If they do order, that only means they will stay longer and spend more money. Food slows down the absorption of alcohol, meaning he can drink more, and that translates to more sales.

Every contact with the guest is a chance to earn another tip. Lighting a cigarette, replacing a soiled napkin, changing an ashtray before the second cigarette is put out are not only ways to increase tips, but these are the signs of exceptional service.

Often a guest will need change to tip the entertainers. Don't be afraid to ask. When returning change from a purchase, always offer extra one-dollar bills. The change from a twenty for a nine-dollar drink should be eleven ones, not a ten and a one.

Eye contact is imperative. You don't want the guest to feel like he is less important than anything else in the room.

The importance of smiling cannot be stressed enough. One smile will do what a thousand words cannot.

BUILD A CLIENTELE

A regular clientele will increase your bottom line and increase the tips for everyone. Everyone on your staff should learn the art of small talk, learn how to be witty without being catty, learn how to make sure all guests feel welcome and special.

Everyone on your staff should strive to learn the names of every guest and make sure all guests know theirs. If they had a good time, guests might ask for that employee the next time they come in.

People like to go to the places they feel most comfortable, and where they know other people, therefore, your staff should introduce a new guest to club regulars as well as other staff members. This creates a web of contacts. If their favorite bartender or waitress isn't working that night, they will know other employees and guests.

Regulars are friends who come to see you and give you and your staff money. This is one of the few jobs in the world where you can make money hanging out with your friends. Go back and re-read the section titled, "You have a good crowd, now what?"

APPRECIATION

It is because of the guests/audience that you have a SHOW. Without them, your club would be just an empty room. This includes guests who cannot afford bottle service or a large tip as well as the guest who can.

Always thank your guests for coming in and for their purchases and tips, no matter what the amounts. Let your guests know you are glad they are spending their valuable time and money in your establishment. When they leave, thank them again for coming in and invite them back.

This is about appreciating the beer sippers as much as the guests buying bottles of champagne, the little tippers as well as the big tippers. The guest who makes ten million a year thinks nothing of a hundred-dollar tip on a three hundred-dollar bottle of champagne. The guest who makes forty thousand a year and gives you ten dollars is actually giving you four times as much of his money. Treat him well, and the day he gets a raise, so will you. Quarters add up. Every tip is a gift. Never return or question a tip as inadequate. You would never return the pair of socks your grandmother gave you for Christmas because you had better ones in your drawer.

At the risk of repeating ourselves, we will say it again: Stop the shakedown of your guests and your entertainers.

If you get a sports star or a famous musician in your club, treat them well but not at the expense of the guy who comes in every week. In fact, introduce the regular guy to the star. He will never forget it, or your club.

CHAPTER 6 | YOUR SUPPORT STAFF

We have always had great staff, some for more than twenty-five years.

March 17-19, 2003, Denver saw one of the biggest blizzards since historical records started in 1872. This classic "Spring Storm" dumped almost 32 inches of very wet and heavy snow on Denver. A manager and DJ took an entire day to clear the snow off the roof, avoiding what could have been a cave-in disaster putting two hundred people out of work.

If it hadn't been for staff loyalty, we would never have won the city council seats needed to keep the club open in the late nineties.

Sometimes we just have fun. Like the time a bartender had a brand new truck and was reluctant to valet. The valet crew felt the bright red truck was vulnerable to being scraped by a passing car being parked in the unsecured area of the lot. To protect the truck, the valet poured water over it throughout the night, building a thick protective layer of ice. At three in the morning, the ice was nearly two inches thick. Normally in Colorado, the temperatures would rise to forty or fifty degrees the next day, but this happened to be a particularly cold week. The truck didn't thaw for five days.

BUILDING A LOYAL STAFF

It's better to train the people you have than to keep hiring new people.
Appreciate the work they do but always demand the absolute best. Look at who is always busy and restocking or cleaning their area. These are the workers you want to keep. Let them know they're doing an excellent job.

A strong, well-oiled team will make money. The more money they make, the more quality you can expect. If your staff is making the best money in town, you can expect them to be the best.

As with playing the music for the crowd you want, you should staff the club for the business you want. If you get surprised by a big bachelor party and you don't have enough staff to handle them, they will tell their friends your service sucks.

If they're slammed, the manager should jump in and help them. It's important that the manager be willing to do everything from answering a phone to taking out the trash. The better you are at staffing and training, the less picking up garbage the manager will have to do; however, when the rush hits, he needs to be willing to jump in and help the staff keep up. The staff will have more respect for the manager, and the manager will have respect for what the staff goes through.

There is a difference between McDonald's, Village Inn, and Del Frescos. It's about the service, not just the number of people through the door when it comes to making money. When everyone works as a team, everyone wins. To have a server steal a guest or a tip today may put an extra fifty in her pocket tonight but cost her hundreds of dollars in the long run. If a coworker is busy, help them through the rush, and they will help you when you need them to go the extra mile.

All staff, and most especially the management team, should make a concerted effort to avoid listening in on guests' conversations unless addressed directly. Avoid engaging guests in extended unnecessary conversation that distracts him from the show. Staff should always remain courteous and friendly with the guests and avoid becoming embroiled in inflammatory conversations. Discussions about politics and religion can often become quite heated. It is far safer to gradually withdraw from the conversation. Taking sides exacts a heavy toll on tips. To become a better conversationalist, a staff member should watch or read the daily news to stay abreast of current events and happenings in sports.

All staff members are required to:

- Greet every customer courteously.
- Recognize good customers immediately.
- Have a complete understanding of all promotions.
- Have a complete understanding of the guest lists as well as the 86 lists.
- Ask each customer if they need change (singles); this puts them in a tipping mood.
- Remain vigilant against selling alcohol to minors or intoxicated guests.
- Be *TIPS* certified or complete a state alcohol service program.
- Continually strive to improve his or her artistic and technical expertise.
- Honor and oblige when intervention is in the public's best interest.
- Handle all monetary transactions in an honest and forthright manner.
- Place composure before their emotions.
- Oversee a legally compliant venue.
- Enforce the dress code.
- Remain sober and alert when representing their employer.
- Work expediently and accept responsibility for their actions.
- Maintain a clean and health-conscious work area.
- Be responsible for the working condition of all equipment in their area.
- Hold no personal prejudices toward any guest, entertainer, or other staff member.
- Provide exemplary service and hospitality.

THE VALET

The valet is usually the first impression a guest has when he visits your club. The valet must be impeccably dressed and polite. He/she should be waiting at the curb for a guest to arrive, not hiding in the key room. If there are multiple valets on duty, there should always be at least one person posted at the front door.

The valet should open the car door and greet the guest with a friendly word and ask if they would like to valet the car.

As guests walk up to the door, the valet should open the door and welcome them to the club with a smile and a "thank you for coming."

In some cases, the valet also serves as security. While a well-trained man in good health can handle almost any tricky situation, a brawny man in a muscle shirt is intimidating and causes guests to wonder if your venue is safe.

The valet should also support your entertainers and staff by helping with luggage and seeing the women safely to their cars at the end of the day.

THE DOOR HOST

The door host is the second, if not the first, employee your guests meet. The impression should be one of professionalism, friendliness, and hospitality. Many bars and nightclubs have no cover charge. The door host sets the tone for the value a guest will receive in your club. He/she should greet every customer courteously and enthusiastically.

When checking I.D.s, they must take the time to make sure everyone is of age. Repeating the guest's name as he/she returns the ID is a friendly gesture to remember the guest.

When a situation arises that entry must be denied for anything other than age, the door host should notify a manager. This is most important if the potential guest is intoxicated. Remember, every interaction with a guest is an opportunity to make a new friend.

The door host may be the only interaction a potential guest has with your company. All telephone calls should be answered with enthusiasm and energy and answered in 2 rings if possible.

THE DJ

A DJ must create a "PARTY" atmosphere with his or her music that is consistent with the club's guidelines and format. Egos are to be left at the front door. He/she must understand that it is not about oneself; it is about a theme and an overall atmosphere.

The light show should add energy without taking away from the entertainer's performance. The rotation should give the guest a variety of entertainers. If possible, have a blond follow a brunette and then follow her with a redhead. Tall women should follow short women to keep the show interesting. Keep in mind that not all girls get along. Try to keep women who dislike each other apart.

He/she should understand the importance of melding entertainers, guests, and music together to generate the necessary energy. This means creating a playlist that can be danced to by a professional entertainer and engages our guests with foot-stomping and applause.

THE BARTENDER /WAITRESS

It is the duty of the server to supply drinks and food to your guests, but don't forget the importance of offering to introduce guests to other guests and to the entertainers. It is by Five Star Service that most tips are earned. Offering a premium drink to a guest isn't being pushy; it's a compliment. It shows that the server thinks the guest has good taste.

We feel that it isn't a good idea to have the entertainers serve drinks or have the waitresses dance on stage. These are vastly different jobs, and not all women are meant to dance or to serve drinks. Although we do allow them to move from department to department, they don't work two jobs at the same time. It would be unfair to the entertainers if a waitress could do a table dance for a guest if she thought she would make a lot of money but not have to dance for a guest who only wanted to pay the set price. And it would rarely make a guest happy if he ordered a drink, and the dancer went on stage instead of bringing his drink.

Bottle service is an entertainment specialty of its own. The server should have plenty of time to spend with the guest and his friends. Your cocktail waitress must be able to perform bottle service and table service that rival five-star, white-glove restaurants. She should be there to pour and garnish every drink. She should not be sitting at the table but be close enough to see if she is needed.

An efficient waitress is a great asset to the team, but the guest comes to your venue to have fun and see beautiful women. Sometimes you will find that two waitresses who are beautiful will make the guest happier than one efficient but unattractive waitress.

TRAINING NEVER ENDS
In the appendix, you will find a sample training manual.

DRINK TICKETS AND ALCOHOL

Here are the basic laws regarding alcohol service and how Shotgun Willie's handles their entertainers.

As a leader in the industry, Shotgun Willie's responds to the need for intelligence and responsibility regarding the consumption of alcohol. Managers must take all necessary steps to educate their staff about alcohol awareness and the applicable laws. Below are some of the major laws that are used nationwide. All of the members of the bar staff are required to maintain current TIPS certification or comparable alcohol awareness training.

SUMMARY OF SHOTGUN WILLIE'S POLICIES AND LAWS

Shotgun Willie's does not:

knowingly allow an intoxicated person into the club.	knowingly allow an intoxicated person to leave with the intention of driving.	"back up" more than 2 drinks.

Shotgun Willie's does:

offer cab service to prevent intoxicated guests from driving.	offer complimentary coffee or food to intoxicated guests in order that time will help to sober them.

Cooperation is needed to maintain an atmosphere of responsible drinking. Staff should notify a manager of any intoxicated persons and take the time to make sure that all their co-workers are aware of the situation. Your primary responsibility is for the safety and wellbeing of your guests. Equally important is your own protection, as the law holds you responsible if you do not adhere to the laws listed below:

It is against the law to serve:

alcohol after or before the times designated by your state.

a known alcoholic at any time.

a disorderly person.

an intoxicated person or anyone who exhibits the following signs of intoxication:

- A change in personality
- Slurred speech
- Loss of coordination
- Irrational statements
- Unable to focus or glassy/bloodshot eyes

any person under the age of 21 or any person who does not have/show one of the following forms of identification:

- Valid state driver's license with photo
- Valid state identification card with photo
- Current military identification card with photo
- Current alien registration card with photo
- Valid passport with photo

Many clubs have been closed for not following the state laws when serving alcohol. These laws pertain to your entertainers and staff as well as your guests.

Because Shotgun Willie's has entertainers under 21, it is imperative that we have strict policies regarding the service of alcohol to entertainers:

We list all entertainers under the age of 21. This list is posted on the reservation sheets so every manager knows who they are.	We put a sparkly wristband on every entertainer who is 21 or older and allowed to drink.	We require each entertainer to ask the manager for a permission slip to give to the bartender or waitress for every drink they have.

You might feel that this is overkill but look at the benefits:

- *The staff will get to know the entertainers by name, making it easier to introduce them to new guests.*
- *The ticket requires managers to speak to their entertainers throughout their shifts.*
- *While writing out the permission slip, the manager can ask how her night is going, ask who she is sitting with, observe her costume, note her demeanor, and, most of all, give her compliments and reassurance.*
- *By complimenting her and asking about her night, she will come to realize the manager really cares about her.*
- *Then, when she needs to be reprimanded for breaking a rule, she will remember all the nice things the manager said earlier.*
- *It doesn't mean she won't scream and pitch a fit, but she will know the manager has her best interest at heart.*

CHAPTER 7 | YOUR MANAGERS

It's always good to care about your staff but don't get taken in by the devious ones.

One February, while on a charity ski trip, one of our managers was standing in the aisle of the bus while it was traveling about sixty miles an hour down the highway.

Unfortunately, the driver had to stop suddenly, and this manager went flying into the front window. The glass fractured but didn't break. He was sore for a few days.

Although the trip raised a lot of money for an entertainer to have reconstructive surgery for a cleft palate, we later discovered she spent the $5,000 on a purebred dog.

We also had a DJ borrow a truck from a manager and disappear for six months.

We aren't always so smart when choosing the people to help, but like our children, we love them anyway.

MANAGERS COME IN ALL SHAPES AND SIZES.

More bars and nightclubs fail due to poor management than all other reasons combined. Some managers have a good working knowledge of inventory and how to control the bottom line but don't have the social skills needed to host a party. Other managers throw a great party but blow all the profits giving away drinks and can't control the pour cost. Some managers come with impressive resumes but are lazy and unwilling to spend the kind of time in the club needed to know what is going on. Some managers are very friendly but can't train or reprimand employees. Some managers are mean and hold themselves so high above the employees they run off talent.

Take the time to search for the right managers for your club. When you find the good ones, hold on to them and pay them well. Below are several qualities to look for in your management team. Since it's extremely rare to find one manager with all the following talents, plan to build a team that has a combination of these qualities and can all get along. Your job as the leader is to train the team so that every member has the appropriate skills.

The good news is that you don't have to rely solely on natural, inborn traits. It is possible to develop the qualities good managers possess. Managers can complete training programs to learn some of the necessary characteristics and can also develop many desirable qualities on their own. At Shotgun Willie's, we use the training programs offered by Walt Disney. The focus of our training has always been creating a culture of fun and gratitude. That isn't to say the following characteristics aren't important, they are, but the most important characteristics a manager can have is a positive and caring attitude.

PERSONAL CHARACTERISTICS

There are traits that can strengthen your manager's abilities and enhance his/her interactions with others. These desirable personal characteristics make a manager someone that others can look up to and feel comfortable following.

Self-Motivation
- An effective manager can't motivate others if he or she can't self-motivate.
- Self-motivation is the ability to get going without outside influence, to take charge of what's next, and is a vital personal characteristic for a manager.

Integrity
- People trust managers who demonstrate personal integrity.
- Workers need to know that their managers will do the right thing, including walking their talk, fighting for their subordinates when needed, and following the rules like everyone else.
- All managers should be dependable and reliable. Both owners and subordinates need to know that the managers can be counted on.

Optimism
- An optimistic attitude can help build morale in your employees.
- A positive attitude can inspire others and help them feel good about getting things done.

Confidence
- A good manager needs to be able to make decisions in confidence and show others that he/she can make good decisions.
- A good manager will take responsibility for his/her decisions.
- Confidence will rub off on others and can be of great benefit.

Composure
- A manager can't afford to break down when the pressure is on.
- The staff will take its cues from the leader. If the manager freaks out in the face of adversity, the staff will be unable to do their jobs.
- Anxiety spreads like wildfire. The ability to remain calm and do what needs to be done is essential in a good manager.

Flexibility
- Managers must stay flexible to adapt to changing situations. Music, drink, and clothing preferences all change over time. (Example: At one time, we couldn't keep Goldschläger on the shelves. Two years later, we couldn't give it away).
- Don't be rigid - it leads to getting stuck in a rut.

BUSINESS CHARACTERISTICS

Some level of business acumen is important for every manager.
Familiarity with basic business principles and practices should be a minimum. Understanding profit and loss, inventory, and sales revenue is crucial to knowing when to go out on a limb and comp that bottle of champagne.

Industry Knowledge
- You and your managers should know everything there is to know about our industry so that you can make good decisions, answer questions, and perform more effectively.
- Take an active interest in the changes in the industry but don't fall for trends.
- If you talk to your guests, you will be able to make the changes needed without investing in unproven ideas.
- Employees may not need extensive industry knowledge, but a manager should have a solid background.

The Ability to Delegate
- Effective managers know that some tasks need to be delegated.
- They should be able to identify workers who will do well and give them tasks at which they can succeed while helping the project.
- Employees will take pride in a job well done, and as the cream rises to the top, you can tap those employees for further promotions.

Organizational Skills
- Good managers need to be organized.
- They must keep track of projects, employees, and assignments.
- They must be on top of the needs of the business.
- Things happen quickly in our business. Trying to remember what time you are meeting someone and where you placed the schedule can be difficult when you have a young woman is in your office crying and a drunk guest picking a fight with the door host.

Basic Money Management
- All managers should understand basic financial concepts.
- Managers should understand how to manage money as part of a project they have been given.
- Managers will be handling a lot of cash. They must know how to balance a safe, how to interpret the daily reading, how to check out the bartenders' tills, how to close the door register and balance the admissions.

Business Hierarchy
- All managers should know how the hierarchy works in your business and follow the chain of command.
- Managers must understand their duties, and to whom they should report.
- If you have mid-level managers, they should know who can tell them what to do and who can't.
- Nothing will confuse your staff faster than having managers overriding each other's decisions.

Understanding the Legal Implications
- While your managers don't need to be experts, they should have a grasp of the legal implications of sexual harassment, proper hiring and firing practices, confidentiality, and more.
- We spend a great deal of time monitoring staff for liquor board violations.
- It is crucial that all your managers interpret and enforce the laws equally.

COMMUNICATION SKILLS

Good managers are able to communicate effectively.
You might be surprised at the different qualities there are related to communication. The following are some qualities managers should possess to be effective communicators.

Writing
- All managers should know how to communicate effectively in writing.
- Good managers can write professionally with correct grammar, and are able to express themselves appropriately in email, memos, and thank you notes.

Public Speaking
- Good managers know how to speak publicly, annunciating words, and concisely communicating ideas, whether speaking with guests or addressing coworkers.
- Being able to succinctly express needs and desires at staff meetings is crucial to running the business.

Coaching Skills
- Knowing how to provide feedback in a way that is helpful to workers and others is one of the most valuable skills managers can possess.
- It is all about getting the results desired. If a manager insults or berates a person, they may do what is asked, but they will do it under duress.
- Managers need to be able to take criticism and coaching as well. We can't say this often enough. There is no place in this business for overblown egos.

Listening Skills

- One of the most important communication skills is being able to really listen.
- Good managers listen to workers, superiors, and guests, and they acknowledge them.
- Good managers repeat back what they've heard said so they can clean up any confusion on the spot, saving time and frustration down the road.

Being Clear and Concise

- When giving instructions, managers must be specific in what is wanted and the expected outcomes.
- Good managers will make sure your employees understand what should happen and why.
- Good managers organize and practice presentations before giving them to keep the agenda or idea clear and concise.
- Presentations that are well thought out will leave little room for miscommunication.

RELATIONSHIP BUILDING

Solid relationship-building skills are possibly the most important abilities a manager should cultivate.

The entire world is built on relationships. Good managers must know how to manage relationships between subordinates, as well as between staff and superiors. They should make employees feel valued. Surveys show that employees want recognition from their superiors. Good managers recognize contributions from all employees.

Respect

- You need to be respectful of your workers if you are to have respect as a manager in return.
- It's up to you to set the example and build relationships of respect.

Guest Service

- Build good relationships with guests if you want your club to be successful.
- Learning how to relate to guests and seeing things from their perspective will engender loyalty and provide the business with the feedback needed to keep the guests coming back repeatedly.
- Many managers make the mistake of thinking that if a guest doesn't complain, then he must be happy. It's important to personally know your guests and what they like and or expect from your business.

Mediator

- Good managers are trained in conflict resolution and will often have to act as mediators between workers, between workers and clients, or between superiors and workers.
- Every interaction with an employee or guest is an opportunity to improve the bottom line.
- When a conflict arises between an entertainer and a guest, everything must be done to make both parties feel good.
- This can be the most difficult part of any manager's job.
- People will lie, and it is difficult to know whom to believe.
- Separate the two parties and do your best to find a happy medium.
- Sometimes you will have to give the guest a free drink or give his money back.
- Sometimes you will have to let an entertainer go home or pay her out of the safe.
- The goal is to have the entertainer continue working at your club and to have the guest come back again.

Team Player

- Your managers need to be able to function as part of a team to succeed.
- Make sure that each one is willing to work with others and respect them.
- Because managers will need to set up collaborations with their own team, they should also be able to work well with others and understand how to integrate ideas and personalities.
- Remember: no single manager could possess all the qualities needed to run a successful club. This is where teamwork comes in.

BUILDING YOUR MANAGEMENT TEAM

If your management team does not have the innate skills to manage their staff, you will be spending much more time running interference than you had planned.
Understanding your team will help you communicate with them as well as teach them how to work together. Below is an overview of the distinct types of people you will employ. There are four basic personalities: Circle, Square, Triangle, and the Squiggle. Good teamwork needs all the shapes.

Squares

Build the systems to get the details done. Your work horse.
These are solid based citizens. They carry the responsibilities of the organization and do the work to get things done. A square will want specifics or perhaps details in writing.

Triangles

Focus on decisions and results. Your bookkeeper.
They are intellectual thinkers who say "Prove it" or "Put it in writing". They are the organized ones. A triangle won't appreciate indecisiveness and are the foundation of you organization.

Circles

Create peace and harmony. Your mediator.
They won't rock the boat and they keep things running smoothly. A circle needs to connect and have a conversation often putting too much emphasis on the things like planning breaks or lunch.

Squiggles

Generate creativity and ideas. Your visionary.
They are dreamers who love change. They come up with the idea but usually let the squares do the work. You may have to remove distractions before getting a squiggle's attention.

 SQUARE:
Systems People

- extremely hard workers
- good long-range planners
- task-oriented, loyal, and organized
- think sequentially and logically
- fond of statistics and graphs
- some can be stubborn with opinions based on their data
- will know policies & rules
- not fond of change, prefers a stable environment
- prefer working alone to teamwork
- they may see fun as unnecessary or a luxury
- they do not like surprises.

 TRIANGLE:
Results People

- they are bottom-line people; focused on goals
- driven to succeed; motivated by results; take charge/move fast
- smart and know a little about a lot of different things
- big-picture oriented
- don't like to be bogged down with details
- competitive, outspoken; can be impatient
- they love to debate and argue, sometimes knocking heads with rivals
- wanting to be right in everything they will rarely admit when they're wrong
- thrive on recognition and put stock in status symbols.

 CIRCLE:
People People

- empathetic and perceptive; fun-loving
- they usually listen and communicate well
- peacemakers, they avoid conflict or making unpopular decisions
- can't say no and are better at caring for others than caring for themselves
- overcommit, taking on more than they can handle, often leaving projects unfinished
- can be easily swayed by opinions of others making them a target for power-hungry and/or lazy co-workers
- they usually enjoy working with other people and being on committees or teams
- don't particularly like hierarchy but are often the glue of the team.

 SQUIGGLE:
Idea People

- often visionaries; creative with lots of energy and enthusiasm; like to try new ways and different things; can appear a little flaky; may have difficulty with completion of projects
- tend to start a task and move on to the next idea before the first gains ground
- can be frustrating to work with
- flexible and spontaneous; easily bored
- make cognitive leaps, from A straight to F
- prefers a less structured environment and has difficulty staying focused
- has great ideas but is terrible when it comes to the budget or following a plan

No matter what you chose
as your favorite shape,
you will need all the personalities
to make a strong team.

Can you imagine if everyone was a *circle*?
You can't sail far in calm waters.

If we were all *squiggles* we would
have trouble staying on course.

All *triangles* and we would spend
all our time charting the course.

Squares may sound ideal but a crew
constantly loading cargo will never set sail.

When the *Squiggle* says
"If we dream it we can build it!"
and the *Triangle* says,
"It's not in the budget!"
The *Circle* will resolve the conflict
and the *Square* will build the dream.

CHAPTER 8 | MANAGING THE UNMANAGEABLE

We have had many occasions where we have had to discipline an employee or a guest. Asking someone to quit drinking and go home can become a tense situation.

One intoxicated guest didn't want to leave and was ignoring the female manager who was trying to get him into a taxi. In a moment of desperation, she grabbed his hands and placed them on her breasts. He was more than happy to follow her, holding her breasts right out the door.

On another occasion, a manager, dressed in a pink bunny costume for Easter, wanted a guest to leave, but the guest got angry and refused. The manager then turned around and started hopping toward the door, telling the guest to follow the bunny. The guest started laughing and followed the manager out. The manager offered the guest a pass to come back the next night, and he has been a regular guest since that night.

We have a time-out stool in the office and a boob hat when an employee does something dumb. We never take ourselves too seriously, except when it comes to service.

To let the wait staff know they have missed a guest, the manager carries brightly colored napkins to place before a guest who has had to wait too long. When the waitress sees this, she knows the manager is paying attention, and the guest isn't the wiser.

MANAGEMENT STYLES

The following are some broad overviews of a selection of management styles and when to use them.

There are thousands of books written on the subject of managing employees. The Three Minute Manager is simplistic in design. It breaks down to: pat them twice, slap them once. A simple compliment or acknowledgment of a job well done will make an employee much more receptive when the time comes to correct or reprimand. We've all heard the saying you'll catch more flies with honey than with vinegar. The only caveat here is the compliment must be sincere. Employees have a sixth sense when it comes to being patronized.

While this management style works in ninety percent of all situations, it is good to have a few tricks up your sleeve. As an owner, it is essential to understand the management styles of those you hire. While all of these examples work, some are not good for you or your club. Below are some samples from a book titled *Management by Guilt*. This paperback is complete with sample scenarios and a self-test. While we won't go into all the styles, below are a few examples of when and how to use different techniques.

As you will see, there are ways to manage different situations, some better than others. Good managers are worth the money because lousy managers will cost you much more than their salaries; they might cost you your license.

Management by Guilt
- one of the original management styles invented by God; "I told you not to eat that apple," and humans have been feeling guilty ever since.
- In our business, you will find most young women have an innate sense of fairness.
- You can often ask a favor of someone you "have dirt on" by reminding the employee that they messed up, and you let them off the hook.

Management by Bribery
- I will pay you more money if you do your job.
- If you are on time to work, I won't charge you house fees.
- While this is one of the easiest ways to get what you want from your staff, be aware: you will eventually run out of money.

Management by Confrontation
- This should always be done in front of other staff.
- No one likes to be singled out for doing something wrong.
- "I don't like the shoes you're wearing, go home."
- You can bet the rest of the staff will think twice about the shoes they wear.
- This should only be used when dealing with "Bad Apples" and thieves.

Management by Example
- Most of the information in this book is centered on being the best manager you can be.
- The example you set for your club is what you will end up with at the end of the day.
- Remember, if you are always late, your staff will be late.
- If you are rude to a guest, your staff will be rude.
- If you come in dressed sloppy, your staff will, too.
- If you walk over trash in the parking lot, so will your staff.

Management by Sensitivity and Listening
- Throughout this book, we stress the importance of talking to and knowing your staff.
- When you know that Mary likes to work Wednesdays, you make an effort to accommodate her needs.
- When you know that Cindy just broke up with her boyfriend, you take a little extra time with her.
- Tell her she's special, pretty, smart, whatever you know will raise her spirits.
- In an uncaring world, listening is invaluable.

Management by Chaos

- Bad managers use this technique a lot.
- A manager who wants to change things every week might be hiding something.
- The staff and numbers are all over the place, going in different directions so the owners can't pin them down.
- This kind of manager will keep other managers and employees on edge because they don't know what change will happen next.
- Chaos Managers are usually control-freaks and tend to be your hardest workers.
- Chaos Managers will have a hand in everything because they don't want anyone really knowing what's going on.
- Because no one knows the boat is sinking, they keep working hard and let this guy pilot the ship.

Management by Baseball

- Sometimes things happen that are out of your control.
- The staff will get anxious if the manager doesn't show concern.
- Like the manager that goes out to settle down the pitcher who is throwing balls, he knows he can't fix it, but he huddles with the pitcher.
- They might be talking about going out for a drink, but the other players see the manager taking action and immediately relax.
- The staff feels like things will get better.

Management by Genius

- Knowing everything that there is to know about the business gives you an edge.
- Your staff will like learning from you and will become a stronger staff.
- Even the simple things like teaching a bartender how to make a new drink or an entertainer how to apply her make up will make employees want to work for you.

Management by Intimidation

- This is similar to management by confrontation but not as effective.
- There is a healthy amount of fear an employee should have about losing his/her job.
- Not because the boss is a heartless jerk who throws his title around, but because it's a really good job.
- The intimidation manager might have limited success for a short while, but soon, you will witness ever-increasing turn-over.

Management by Intrigue
- Wouldn't it be interesting if we tried this or that?
- This kind of manager is always coming up with new ideas.
- Some of these have validity and should be explored.
- If the change in policy is just to see how people will react, you might be shooting yourself in the foot.
- Change for the sake of change is a waste of energy.

Management by Management
- Always having the right answer and being in the right place at the right time.
- If you do your best every day, you end up managing well.
- Employees like working for good managers.
- Keep in mind, it's almost impossible to keep up, and you will have to resort to some of the other tactics on occasion.

Management by Seduction
- Much like bribery, seduction is a reward for good behavior.
- The rewards don't have to be monetary; in fact, it is better if you don't use money.
- Reward good behavior with accolades and better shifts.
- Being a part of a happy family is a great reward for a job well done.

Management by Revenge
- We all know the laws regarding retaliation. It isn't uncommon to have a staff lie about what a manager has done or not done in fear of retaliation.
- It isn't limited to sexual harassment but includes everything from trading services for comp tickets to arguing/fighting with guests. "Since you made me look bad, I'll give you jobs or a schedule that I know you'll hate."
- A good manager will set his ego aside in defense of the business.

Management by Deceit
- Flat out lying about what an employee will get if they do what you say is a prime example of management by deceit but not the only way it can be used.
- Sometimes you can tell your staff a liquor board member is in the building to help clean up the dance area.
- You might tell a guest the police are on the way to hurry him into the taxi you provided.
- You might tell an employee he/she is the best person for the job to "seduce" them into doing something they didn't really want to do.

CHAPTER 9 | YOUR FACILITY

Don't underestimate the power of synergy.

When your venue is located within walking distance of several other nightclubs and restaurants, you create synergy, and such is the popularity of entertainment districts.

When people go out for the evening, they often visit two or more places: dinner, a movie, and a drink, for example.

It is more likely a new guest will visit your club if they are in the neighborhood already.

Your vision is to become a must-hit venue on the patrons' list. Planning joint promotions with the clubs and restaurants in your neighborhood can increase traffic for all.

It might even be advantageous to locate your entertainment club next to a club of a similar type. Just make sure your facility is distinctive enough to appeal to a diverse demographic.

A typical guest will spend anywhere from thirty minutes to two and a half hours in a venue depending on many factors, including entertainment, seating, service, and concept.

REMODELING OR DESIGNING A NEW VENUE
Rule of thumb: don't let a salesman design your club.

The interior of your venue is vital to your success or failure. The best club layouts will encourage patrons to socialize; after all that's why people go out. You want to promote social interaction for your patrons who want to feel comfortable and have an enjoyable time. If you just throw-in expensive and cool looking objects to impress your guests, without regard to the comfort and flow of the room, you will only end up turning them off. Witness the number of popular local bars that stay in business while high-dollar, extravagant hot-spots fade in less than a year.

Begin with some basic strategies.
The flow of the room is crucial. A guest will want to be able to navigate your venue with ease and enjoy a variety of spaces and entertainment. Creating eye contact and promoting social interaction is a huge factor in developing human relations. You want to create connections between patrons. A male patron will want to walk by a female without committing himself to an introduction. When you have a single aisle through the center of your club with all the action along the walls, patrons will feel they are on exhibition as they make their way to a seat. Once there, they won't want to get up to use the restroom.

Setting entertainment in several locations with paths winding throughout the room will allow the guest to stroll around the perimeter, gaze at the other patrons and entertainment and look as if he is just passing by. This is also ideal for your entertainers. This gives them the opportunity to pass many guests, making eye contact, and smiling without appearing to be on a runway or on the prowl.

Having many different areas provides the guest with a variety of places to sit and provides the guest with attachment points. An attachment point is a place the guest can "home in on" and feel safe and/or comfortable. Over the years, we have seen countless regulars sit at the same table or on the same barstool every time they came in. These are attachment points. The more attachment points you create in your venue, the more comfortable your guests will feel.

Examples of good attachment points are:

a booth, couch, or chair	**a table or high-top table**
a bar top, drink rail, pony wall or railing	**a platform in the form of a stage with seating**

Examples of poor attachment points are:

a structural column	**a wall**	**air**

As we are talking about stages as attachment points, keep in mind that this is how your entertainers make money. If you want your club to be successful, your entertainment stages must be comfortable. Many guests get up and follow an entertainer from stage to stage, but if the next entertainer on stage is exciting, the guest will stay seated, and this means more time and money spent in your club. Stages are like communal tables in a nightclub. The idea of the communal table is a place to meet new people and share the experience. Your staff can magnify the effect of the party by facilitating the introduction of guests to one another.

A significant part of your planning should include your staff. You can have the most beautiful club, but if the waitress can't get from the bar to the guest in a reasonable time, you are going to fail. If given the opportunity, invite a bartender and waitress to sit in on your design phase. They will often spot a failure in the design before you spend thousands of dollars. Several design companies specialize in bars and nightclubs. Before you hire one, visit a few of their projects. Ask the staff about how functional the design is. Rest assured, they will tell you what does and doesn't work, and you can avoid mistakes.

You can get competitive prices on liquor if you buy it by the case. Make sure you have adequate dry and cold storage space for your liquor, bottled, and draft beer. You'll want these products in a lockable space where you can control the inventory. Also plan space for cases of back-up glassware, napkins, straws, juices, and bag-in-the-box sodas.

When designing your entertainers' dressing room, you'll want to have it well ventilated. Ladies use a variety of perfumes, and dance shoes can have a scent all their own. We use gym lockers to help mitigate the build-up of odors. These open steel lockers also allow the manager to see what's inside, discouraging entertainers from bringing in liquor and drugs.

Carpeting holds odors that can include feces, urine, and vomit and will have to be replaced often. Save yourself some money and put down some nice vinyl.

Your house mom/locker room manager will have to have a place to set up where she has an unobstructed view of the room. Design a place for a make-up artist, hairstylist, and costume sales. If you want your entertainers to be the best in the business, provide them with the tools. With contract leasees, you can't tell them what they can wear, but you can control what costumes are sold on your property.

Drunks will be incredibly hard on your club. You will wish you had built everything of steel and cement. Where possible, like the restrooms, use polished colored concrete or tiles. Having hot water hose bibs behind all the bars allows you to spray down the bar once a week, keeping mold and bar rot at bay. Hardwood is expensive but will hold up longer than pine. Avoid pressed board at all costs. Moisture will eventually destroy everything, but laminates and pressed boards will succumb quicker.

Spend the money to have a great sound system, good lighting, and buy good furniture but be aware these things will have to be replaced often.

Once you have located your venue, you need to ensure you have ample well-lit parking. You don't want chilly weather or paid parking to send patrons to another club. Having security patrol the lot will encourage patrons to stop at your club first. It's up to you to keep them.

MAINTAINING A TOP-NOTCH CLUB
You can't fix what you can't see.

Let's start with your daily maintenance. Have you looked at a picture and asked yourself, "What's wrong with this picture?" Maybe it was just crooked or out of place. Maybe the picture was just the wrong color or size. Or maybe you just didn't like the picture itself. We have all had these experiences. If you think about it, life is a series of pictures that we perceive with our eyes.

This makes up the world we see. Some are good pictures, some are bad, and some are indifferent. For most of us, when we see a good picture, we stop for a moment and enjoy the scene. With a bad picture, we usually turn and walk away because we don't like what we see. The picture that is indifferent, we don't judge at all.

All these pictures we are seeing are just our own thoughts, manifesting in our world of perception. To make this basic, if you carry around negative thoughts, you will see a negative world. If you carry around positive thoughts, you will see a positive world. The truth is, we all carry around both positive and negative thoughts every day. Therefore, the world that we see is a mixture of good and bad images or pictures. There is an Eastern saying, "If you want to change the world, change your thoughts about it."

As a club manager, you are responsible for the images and pictures the public sees. In many ways, you are the club curator. Webster's dictionary defines curator as an overseer; one that takes care of; an administrator. So, as a good curator, you must make sure the picture you present to your guests is as pleasing as possible. Every day as managers, we view hundreds and hundreds of pictures, and so does each guest. As you know, the pictures and images that your guests see make the difference between them coming back to your club or not. Now, as a manager (curator), you can determine the kinds of pictures and images your guests see. You might think you can't control everything you see, but the truth is you need to, or what you see will control you.

There is a technique called "focused viewing," which, when mastered, puts you in control of your inner camera, which, of course, is your eyes. Focused viewing is nothing more than breaking down the picture you view to smaller frames or smaller pictures. For example, if you are looking at the main bar area, focus your eyes to bring in a smaller picture of this bigger area. As you view this smaller frame, ask yourself, "What is wrong with this picture?"

This is the most important question you can ask throughout your shift. The big picture is important but only in relation to the smaller frames that compose it. Maybe as you focus on this smaller frame, you see a dirty ashtray, an empty bottle, or even a dirty bar towel on the bar. Maybe you see a torn barstool or a broken shelf. When you look at the big picture, these details are lost.

Another example might be viewing the door or entryway from a distance. From this view, everything looks in order; however, when you reduce the picture to a smaller frame and ask yourself what is wrong, you see the details that make up the larger picture. Is the door host dressed properly? How do his shoes look? Is he smiling?

Choose another frame. Is the counter clear of clutter? Are the boutique items displayed neatly? Or another. Is the lighting bright enough? Are there any burned-out bulbs? Are the signs hung correctly? Are the signs outdated?

As you continue to view these smaller pictures, you will discover the details of your club that only these smaller pictures will uncover. Remember, when you view the larger picture, everything seems in order. FOCUSED VIEWING is your answer to taking care of the details.

The first rule is to break all pictures into smaller pictures and then ask the question, *"What is wrong with this picture?"* The second rule is; always fix a frame that doesn't look right. Never, ever leave a picture that doesn't look right.

If it doesn't look right, change it. Change it now.

If you use this focused viewing technique, you will be amazed at the various kinds of pictures you will see. By using this technique, you can take care of the big picture that your guests will see, and it will be a pleasing one.

Train yourself to become a good curator. Keep taking these little snapshots as you view your club. As you get better at taking these little snapshots, your club will get better, too.

An effective way to train for focused viewing is to do it with another manager. Walk together for a short distance, looking at these smaller pictures. Compare the pictures each of you saw. See if they were the same. If they are not the same, keep practicing. It is only through practice that you will get better. Don't forget, focused viewing applies to everything and everyone you see. You are the curator; the overseer; the one who takes care of things. We promise you will never run out of pictures.

CHAPTER 10 | SECURITY

 A good-looking man walks into a bar. He has a tiny man sitting on his shoulder. He reaches into his pocket and pulls out a $50 bill and buys a round for the house. Moments after the bartender sets up the drinks, the little man jumps down and kicks over all the cocktails.

The handsome man pulls out another fifty, and the bartender sets up another round. Again, the little man kicks over all the drinks. This happens three more times before the bartender says, "I'm not pouring another drink until you tell me what's going on here."

The handsome man says, "You see, I found this magic bottle with a genie inside who offered me three wishes. First was to be handsome."

The bartender nodded. "Yes, you are pretty good looking."

"The second wish was to find a fifty dollar bill every time I reached into my pocket."

"I see," said the bartender.

"Lastly, I asked for a twelve-inch prick, and here he is, right on my shoulder."

THE BEST SECURITY IS GOOD RELATIONSHIPS

If you are handling your club with finesse, and if you are making relationship-building a policy and training priority, you can turn a problem guest into a loyal guest. *Every interaction with another person is an opportunity to win loyalty.*

As a rule, managers and staff should be taking care of guests, particularly the ones you have overserved. *The best protection against fights is not having to deal with an unruly guest.*

You can achieve this by being in touch with all your guests and training your staff to come to you if a problem arises. Remember, a difficult person can be controlled while an unruly person cannot be controlled.

When a guest has overindulged or hit the limit on his credit card, calling the local police should always the last resort, and you should not rely on the police to clean up your mess.

With that said, we all know there's always the possibility of a guest who becomes a public safety threat, and then you will have to call the police. Other guests, the general public and the police, will appreciate the effort to handle the situation with little or no violence whenever possible.

WHAT IS AN UNRULY PERSON?

An unruly person is a person who is interfering, through verbal and/or physical actions, with the rights of another person to enjoy themselves or to do their job and are challenging to control. This could be something as simple as an insult or a vicious as an assault. It is not possible to cover all the varied and tricky situations that could develop with this type of person. However, we can give you some sensible guidelines to follow for deescalating a situation.

Never, ever strike or hit a guest or employee unless you are protecting yourself or another from immediate serious harm.

If someone is physically assaulting you or threating you or another with a knife or a gun, you must protect yourself, then restrain or hold the person until help arrives.

Striking or assaulting a person can never be justified unless the above conditions are met.

If you have to protect yourself from an assault it means we did something wrong.

We want to avoid this type of situation if at all possible.

Before a person becomes unruly, he is usually difficult. A difficult person is one who is hard to please, satisfy, or manage. And this usually happens when a person has had too much to drink, is under the influence of drugs, or both.

- **Learn to identify a person who is difficult before they become unruly.**
  - A person becomes difficult because something has happened to cause him/her to become angry.
  - This could be an argument, an illness, or even an accident.
  - There could be any number of things that may have happened to him/her earlier in the day that we are not aware of, and that may have caused this person to become difficult.
- **Drugs and alcohol may bring this anger to the surface.**
  - Under these conditions, it is quite human to take out one's anger and frustration on those around them.
  - People tend to project their anger and frustration outward to get rid of them.
  - Of course, this never works and usually makes things worse.
  - People who are difficult are really just making a call for help. They may need someone to listen and confide in so they can vent their feelings.

- **Do not personalize any words or actions coming from a difficult person.**
  - To do so is to lose control of the situation entirely.
  - Losing control is what the difficult person wants you to do. In his/her mind, it gets the monkey off their back, and now they have cause to attack you.
- **Stay calm.**
  - Never scream, swear, or argue with a difficult person. In fact, you should do just the opposite. You should listen, be empathetic, and understanding. When you do talk with this person, you should come across as his friend, not his enemy.
  - This almost always works, although you must be sincere, or the person will see right through you.
  - What you are really attempting to do is make sure this person does not become unruly. You can usually eliminate the situation by solving the person's problem.
  - The easiest way to do this is to listen to what he/she has to say then act accordingly.
- **Much of a manager's job is making people happy.**
  - Being right or wrong is subjective and often hard to discern.
  - You must rely on your common sense to have the best outcome.
- **Look for common ground to explore.**
  - In other words, change the subject.
  - Sometimes, talking about sports, girls, guys, or even telling a good joke will ease any tension that remains.
  - This usually helps to get the guest's mind off the problem and puts you in the position of being his friend.
- **Don't think you have all the answers because you don't.**
  - You will learn new things with every guest you meet.
  - If you're having a hard time getting the situation resolved, it might be best to let another person take over the conversation.
  - Another manager or employee might have a better rapport with this person.
- **There are always exceptions to what we call "the gray area."**
  - An unruly person will usually be asked to leave our club by a manager, but not always.
  - You, as a manager, must make the decision, and sometimes you will have to make this decision without prior experience with the situation you're in at that moment.

Notice that we said, "asked him/her to leave our club." We did not kick or throw them out. Once you make the decision to ask someone to leave, they must leave. When informing a guest that he/she must leave, be as polite and understanding as possible but stay firm. If possible, talk to this person privately. Ask him/her to follow you as you walk away and always toward the front door.

The guest should follow you right out of the club, which is your goal, as a situation can be handled more efficiently when you are both away from loud music and other guests. This also does a couple of additional things: It gets him away from friends but does not embarrass him, and usually, another doorman or manager will be there to back you up.

Once outside, explain why he/she is being asked to leave. Be courteous. Give the person a moment or two to collect themselves and perhaps finish a cigarette (but not their drink, which may result in an allegation of allowing an intoxicated or disorderly person to continue drinking - thus creating potential liability for the club.)

Offer the person a free ride home if they have had too much to drink.

- There is always another day to party.
- Sometimes offering this person a free pass or a free drink to be used on another day will often dissolve any tension in the air.
- Let the person know there are rules and that you care about his/her safety, your liquor license, and the people who work for you.

Keep your eyes open and be alert to anything he/she might do.

- Once the person is outside turn him over to your Valet or security.
- Do not stand outside and argue; you have a club to run.
- Notify your door personnel not to let the guest back in the club that day/night.

Only call the police if someone is hurt or you have no other choice.

- This is a last resort.
- You may tell the guest you have called, and the police are on the way, but try to resolve this without involving the law.
- The guest will thank you when he sobers up or calms down.

If you want a good working relationship, never hide anything from your local police. If something is getting out-of-hand, call them and give them the "heads-up" at the very least. If you know someone is selling drugs out of his car in your parking lot or across the street, let the police have the bust. It helps keep your club clean and safe while making your local police look good.

If you work with your local police, they will know when they get the call from you that you have done everything in your power to mitigate the problem. A good policeman is a peace officer. They don't want to take your guest to jail any more than you want to turn a guest into an enemy of your club.

Always remember the Golden Rule: treat people the way you would like to be treated.

WHEN DIPLOMACY FAILS

You are always responsible for how you act, no matter how you feel.

- **When a fight breaks out involving two or more persons:**
    - First, alert the security to the location and nature of the incident, then make your way quickly WITHOUT RUNNING to the scene and separate the participants.
    - If a physical assault continues, then you will restrain the participants putting distance between the parties.
    - Identify the aggressor and quickly escort him out of the building and off the premises.
- **When two patrons are being ejected for fighting:**
    - the more aggressive person is ejected first.
    - When he has physically left the premises, the second person should then be ejected.
    - Never let two people out at the same time who have been involved in an altercation to "duke it out."
    - It is inappropriate and just asking for trouble.
- **You are not there to hurt anyone or "KICK SOMEONE'S ASS."**
    - You are there to ensure the safety of all patrons, even those who may be intoxicated, obnoxious, or combative.
    - Remember, it was most likely your staff who over-served the guest.
- **When using your door personnel for security:**
    - The front register cannot be left unattended, so make sure that when a situation occurs, there is someone watching the register.

CHAPTER 11 | MARKETING

The world is an open book when it comes to marketing. We have an annual Large Lady / Voluptuous Vixen strip off every Valentine's Day. During the summer, we throw a White Trash Party complete with old tires and chickens. No public figure goes unscathed with our Hilary, Dolly, and Melania strip-offs. We are known to celebrate the most obscure holidays, including our Girl Scout Cookie eating contests, but our golf tournaments are legendary.

The local news usually gets a camera close enough to have something to show on television, like a clip of one of the managers throwing an entertainer in the lake. That clip must have played two or three times a night for more than a week.

One of our tournaments had one manager run over another manager with the cart, but that was less damage than the time the crew lost a cart in the lake.

We had an entertainer in tears one trip because she tipped a cart over, killing a squirrel.

Although it was stressful, it wasn't as uncomfortable as showing up to the golf course with fifty entertainers, many who had been drinking for the last two hours, on the heels of a junior golfer's tournament.

Yes, the junior golfers were still in the clubhouse, and no, we weren't invited back.

STRATEGIC MARKETING

Keep your eyes on the stars and your feet on the ground.

Running a bar sounds easy. Buy some beer and liquor, put on some music, hire a couple of girls to take their clothes off, and then sit back and watch the money pour in. Well, it doesn't quite work like that. You have one chance to earn a solid clientele. If you deliver a poor product, it will cost three times the marketing dollars to win back those same clients.

Marketing is vital for any business.

The development of a marketing plan takes thorough consideration. As strategic thinkers, we're always searching for a competitive edge.

Your marketing strategy should:

<table>
<tr>
<td>Develop long-term profitable relationships with your customers.</td>
<td>Be flexible and responsive to changes in customer demands.</td>
<td>Identify and communicate the benefits of your business.</td>
</tr>
</table>

Your marketing plan should address these three questions:

<table>
<tr>
<td>Where is the business now?</td>
<td>Where do you want to be?</td>
<td>How best can you get there?</td>
</tr>
</table>

It's not enough to create the plan; you must monitor its effectiveness and make any adjustments required to maintain its success. It takes time and effort to develop and maintain marketing campaigns that resonate.

Your marketing plan is a vital part of your budget. Set aside no less than 10% of your working capital to bring people into your club. The key to a good promotion is to be inventive, not expensive. You must spend money to make money but maybe not as much as you think. Warning: web searches for things like tiny strippers or drag queens will bring a "pornado" of unwanted adult ads to your inbox.

MARKETING CAMPAIGN TIPS

While overall marketing strategy is a long-term endeavor, don't get caught up in running a successful promotion too long.

A large part of any campaign is in its freshness and uniqueness. Ladies night isn't a new idea but your spin on it will make all the difference.

Never underestimate the power of the short run. If you have cheap drinks every Monday you will attract a crowd for several weeks. Once the crowd realizes this will happen every Monday, they are less inclined to make a point of hitting your club. Scarcity motivates action.

Special events and promotions should always feature your entertainers. That is the real business you're in, not alcohol sales.

THE FIVE BASIC FORMS OF MARKETING

Partnerships/Affinity

Word of Mouth/In House Promoting

Social Media - Text/Email/Google

Guerrilla Marketing/Out of House Opportunities

Traditional Public Relations

Partnerships/Affinity

A joint venture is formed between two or more businesses to pool resources in an effort to promote and sell products and services.

Create strategic partnerships that are mutually beneficial by forming alliances with complementary brands.

Also known as partnership marketing, with this strategy, one brand generates sales while the other creates new customers and builds brand awareness.

Word of Mouth/In House Promotions

The least expensive and most far-reaching advertising should be done in the club. If you have twenty people in the club and you can get them to come back with a friend, you have doubled your guest count. How do you do this? Give them a reason to visit every day. On-the-spot parties are personal and cheap.

Birthday Parties and Bachelor Parties are a given. Try adding Graduation, Retirement, or Promotion Parties.

Games are great mixers during the day but can get lost late night. Service Industry Night is popular for slower nights.

Dress up days – like Comic-Con, Halloween, and Prom Night can involve your support staff as well as the entertainers.

Every Valentine's Day we pay tribute to more voluptuous women with our popular Large Lady Strip-off.

For the entertainer we have Rear of the Year, Best Breast in the West, Foxy Boxing, and Mashed Potato Wrestling, to name a few.

We host impersonation strip-offs such as Dolly Parton, Hilary Clinton, and Melania Trump. Anyone in the news is fair game.

Feature of the Month is a little more complicated but gives your entertainers a chance to really shine.

A note about giving away drinks: ALWAYS GET SOMETHING BACK.

If you see a guest getting ready to leave, that free drink might encourage him to stay much longer than he had planned.

- At Shotgun Willie's, we often use drinks as a way of buying goodwill when a guest hasn't had a pleasant experience. The caveat is you MUST FIX THE ISSUE.
- Buying off someone who complains without addressing the problem will only cause you to pay over and over for the same issue.
- A round of drinks for your staff after a particularly grueling night is a nice reward. If you do it every night, it will become an expectation, and then you won't have any way to reward the tough shifts.
- When you're out on the town, it's great to offer to buy a drink for someone if they come into your club. Best advice: **Don't** comp both the door and the drink, or you may not make a dime. Although, if he has a really fun time, he'll be back often.
- NEVER buy a drink for a guest who asks for one. Instead, offer to buy the third or fourth round.
- Don't buy a drink for the guy who has a large bar tab. You will only have a drunk to deal with later. Instead, buy him a meal or a dance.

Social Media - Text/Email/Google

These days, when consumers have questions, they often don't ask their friends; they go straight for Google. In fact, Google is so good at answering our questions that millions of people daily search for their answers on this leading Internet search site. One does not have to look far to see the power of search marketing. Google has shaped the industry for many years now and has helped hundreds of retailers grow their businesses.

While many businesses used to advertise in their local yellow pages, as fewer consumers consult their local physical directory, this channel's effectiveness dwindles more each year.

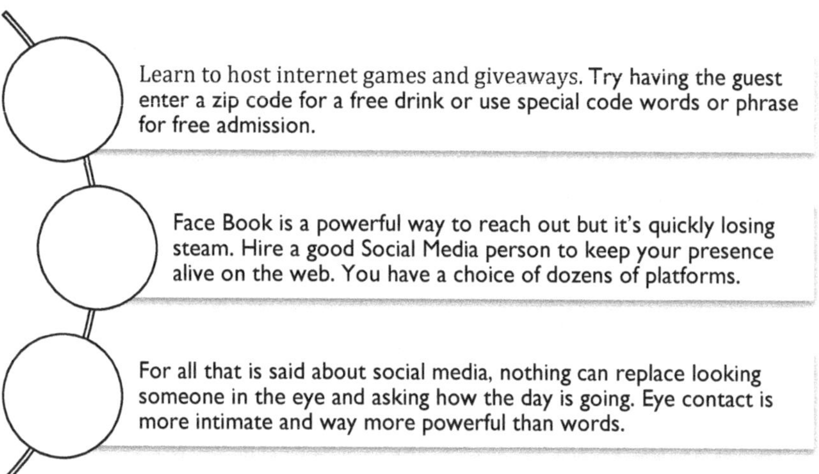

Guerrilla Marketing
Grassroots, untraditional, and low-budget methods that involve creativity, big crowds of people, and the element of surprise. Unlike Freebies and drink giveaways, these are not dependent on complementary marketing, but rather consists of giving away a free sample of the product to influence the consumer to make the purchase. Sending entertainers out to events is a way for new guests to see a sample of what your club offers.

Event examples include:

Trade shows	Parades	Sporting events
Concerts	Bikini contests	Scavenger hunts
Cardboard derbies	Team member bar crawls	

Traditional PR

Radio

- We find the best use of radio is having our girl do guest appearances on the radio or having a hot DJ do a live remote from our club.

Newspaper

- Advertising for a big event can be useful but fewer and fewer people are reading newspapers opting for digital information. Save the dollars here and buy Twitter or Facebook ads.

Trade publications

- Write and publish articles and online content to educate potential customers about your products and services. For the appropriate businesses, this can be an effective means of influencing them without using direct selling methods. In industries where expertise is highly valued, articles can offer a powerful tool to showcase your knowledge and expertise.

Trade shows

- Many products have to be experienced to be bought. Tradeshows are industry gatherings where consumers are invited to sample all that the industry has to offer. Attending trade shows and meeting people in your industry will add to your knowledge of what's new and hot right now.

Mail lists

- You can develop your own mailing lists from your regular clientele. In our industry, we find most of our guests prefer not to have items mailed to their home or office. Email lists are usually more private and much less costly.

Telemarketing

- While many of us dislike telemarketers, this form of marketing can and should include everyone who calls your business. There is a big difference between trying to close a sale on a time-share and asking someone to come in for a free office party.
- Companies often have customers calling them for various reasons. This can present a great opportunity to introduce potential customers to your business.
- When telemarketers call to find out if you are interested in purchasing a new credit card process your door host can invite them in for a party.

MARKETING TOOLS

In each of these forms of marketing, you should consider the best tools to achieve your goals.

These tools include:

Volume Sales	Call to Action	Humanistic
Viral Markets	Diversity	Personalized
Brand Building/Lover	Cause Marketing	Newsletters

Volume Sales

Giveaways and free samples are great for getting the guest in the door. You might try selling some of your products and services at a lower rate to boost the sales of other related products or services such as a free drink with the purchase of a table dance.

Get One Free or Two for One are a commonly used Happy Hour specials but try it with your bottle service and see the sales go up.

Offering food keeps a guest in the club longer and slows down his drinking. Try offering a free appetizer with a bucket of beer.

Call to Action

A call to action is a strategy designed to stimulate a customer to act towards a buying decision.

This technique includes various incentives to buy, such as:

Contests

- We all enjoy winning something for free. Contests offer an attractive marketing vehicle. An added benefit to this tool is interaction with your guests leading to relationship building.

Coupons

- According to the Promotion Marketing Association (PMA) Coupon Council, Over 76% of the population use coupons. Coupons work and provide an affordable marketing strategy for small business.

Sampling

- Try before you buy. Giving your customers a small taste can lead to a big purchase. Liquor companies like to introduce new product. Hosting a party for a new vodka can boost the night's sales.

One Time Offers

- Maybe you're planning to drop a brand of whiskey. This is a great opportunity to increase sales. Running a special on a slow moving whiskey will also clear inventory space for a more popular brand.

Seasonal Specials

- Seasonal specials get the consumer in for an event like Mashed Potato Wrestling, Gift Wrapping, or Feature of the Year. This gives your in house marketing a chance to entice the consumer to come back again.

Humanistic

Human needs are "a state of felt deprivation." They distinguish between physical needs (food, shelter, safety, clothing), social needs (belonging and affection), and individual needs (knowledge, self-expression). Our business centers on the social needs of belonging and having/feeling affection.

- Everyone wants to feel like a VIP. They want to feel like this is their club. By introducing every guest to two or three new people each time they come in, you will create a spider web of connections.
- You might not have thought about the humanistic value of the upsell. Here, offering a guest a premium brand of vodka when he didn't mention one by name isn't being pushy, it's saying you look like the kind of man who drinks Ketel One or Absolut.

Viral market

When something exciting happens, everyone will talk about it. The stranger it is, the more chance it has of going viral.

It's not enough to have the prettiest girls or the best show in town. You must set yourself apart by doing the unexpected, by putting something on your marque that causes people to talk.

Diversity Marketing

As we have said before, cater to a diverse crowd for mass appeal, and don't forget the women who enjoy your entertainment.

The same guy who likes Mashed Potato Wrestling might not be interested in the MILF Strip Off. Golf outings don't draw the same crowd as a charity ski trip. Service Industry Night will draw its own crowd.

Personalized Marketing

Personalized marketing is ideally one-to-one marketing. Personalization creates a unique product for each customer.

Locker Programs provide a guest with the opportunity to order a product you don't carry and is a notable example of personal marketing. Add to that, golf outings, ski trips, birthday and office parties. Anything you can do for an individual to make him feel special will engender loyalty.

Brand Lover Marketing

Develop raving fans by being "the place to be" every night of the week. For a brand to elevate itself into the "Cult Brand" category, it has to give consumers a feeling of belonging while generating strong feelings of love for its consumers.

This requires emotional connections that generate the highest levels of love and a sense of belonging for your brand. We have developed special seating areas for our locker members and the A-Listers who drop by. We don't have any truly isolated areas because of the temptation to do naughty things, but we have areas set apart where a guest can feel special and still be part of the action.

It's not unusual to have reservations for the *Play Pen, Nook, or the Corner of Broken Dreams* weeks in advance.

A note of warning: Your raving fans can be a real pain. They will start feeling as if they own the place. They will make demands you can't accommodate. They may expect your entertainers to meet them outside the club for other social events. They will toss around the owner's name as if they were investors or first cousins. They will claim a table or barstool and challenge anyone who might want to sit there.

Cause Marketing

We host two regular events each year, our Golf Tournament and our Feed the Homeless dinner. These events give our staff the joy of being altruistic. There is nothing like seeing a child's eyes light up when you give him a toy or a man, down on his luck, eating for the first time in days.

Our entertainers are happy to do Dollar Dances (a 30-second dance at a table for a dollar) to help raise money for the homeless, for *Toys for Tots*, for a co-worker in need, or for a battered women's shelter.

You might not think of this as marketing, but when people hear how generous our staff is, they are glad to spend their own dollars with us.

Newsletters

A fun way to promote a business is to write a newsletter that highlights some of the newsworthy things that have happened for the organization.

These newsletters create a sense of inclusion and participation with employees, providing a sense of belonging and something to share with guests.

Sample Promotions

Below are some promotions we have tried with various results. Always keep it fresh. Surprise your regular guests with something new and exciting every time they come in.

Kopy Kats featured several entertainers doing impersonations.

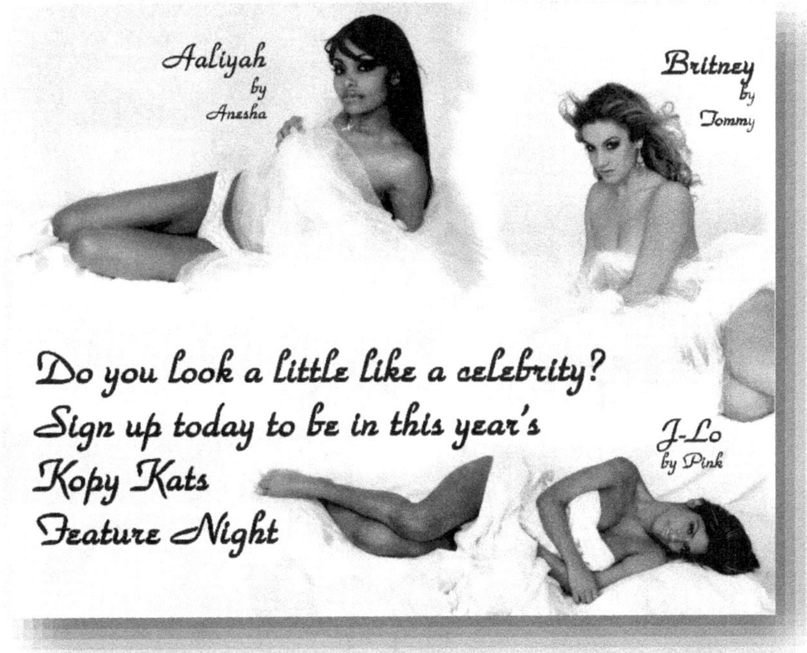

SHOTGUN WILLIE'S
EST. 1982
DENVER COLORADO
Join us for a Story Book Party
On Wednesday, September 17th
Test your knowledge of fairytales playing Strip Trivia for cash & prizes
490 S. Colorado Blvd
Glendale, CO 80246
303-388-9601 · shotgun-willies.com

Chocolate Syrup Wrestling
SHOTGUN WILLIE'S
EST. 1982
GLENDALE COLORADO
WEDNESDAY, SEPT 17TH AT 10:00

CHAPTER 12 | ACCOUNTING & FINANCIALS

 Open the doors and watch the money flow in. Well, not exactly.

Every business has unique particulars that set it apart. In this day of credit cards, most businesses don't keep a lot of cash on hand. Then again, most businesses won't have a guest who regularly tips his waitress $20,000. One of our well known "high rollers" usually spends $50,000 to $100,000 every visit. Your entertainers won't be happy if they have to wait until the end of the month to get paid.

We have ATMs onsite for those guests who don't carry cash but wish to tip an entertainer who doesn't take credit cards. Making it "Rain" one-dollar bills on a stage means having to have one-dollar bills available.

Every business needs a reliable system of tracking inflows (Income; Accounts Receivable) and outflows (Expense; Accounts Payable) to determine profit or loss and overall financial health of the business, including cash flow, assets, and liabilities. The principles, policies, and systems employed are usually based on generally accepted accounting principles and involve the services and skills of both bookkeepers and accountants.

BOOKKEEPING IS A FUNCTION OF ACCOUNTING.

Your bookkeeping staff, whether it is one person or ten, will be responsible for tracking, recording, and reporting on the daily, weekly, monthly, quarterly and annual transactions - both inflows and outflows.

Your Accountant (CPA) will take the bookkeeper's reports and use those numbers to prepare and file your tax returns each year. An accountant will also provide other valuable services to your club.

DEVELOP A BUDGET

Your budget sets the expectations of your revenue and expense. Are you opening a new club? Be sure you have enough capital to cover expenses and stay afloat for an entire year.

REVIEW YOUR BUDGET-TO-ACTUAL NUMBERS FREQUENTLY

Things happen ridiculously fast in this industry. Three down weeks is a trend. If you only look at the net numbers once a quarter, you could be out of business before the numbers come out.

Shotgun Willie's closes their books at the end of every month, balancing the cost of goods and services to income. They keep a close watch on the beer, wine, and liquor PC (percent cost). They strive to have less than 2% loss on all liquor/beer, or a 98% PC.

If your gross numbers are usually in the high nineties and they start slipping into the low nineties, take a close look at your staff. If you have a bartender or manager stealing $500.00 a night, four nights a week, you will lose $8,000.00 in a month. If you settled your accounts just once a quarter, you would have already lost $24,000.00. If you close your books at the end of the year, you would have lost $96,000.00 before you realized you had a thief.

SAMPLE BUDGET

A sample budget might look like this:
All these categories can be broken down into sub-categories, making it easier to track expenses.

Cost of Goods Sold	20%
Fixed Expenses	20%
Management	18%
Payroll	13%
Administration	12%
Promotions and Advertising	10%
Supplies and Maintenance	07%

- For instance, Cost of Goods can be broken down into alcohol, wine, bottled beer, and draft beer, food, cigars, and boutique sales.
- Break your payroll down by department and split out the costs of insurance and taxes. This will help you keep your payroll in line.
- You will have regular bar supplies like straws and glassware and ongoing maintenance like furniture replacement.
- We've already discussed the distinct types of advertising. This is another place that tends to creep up if not diligently watched.
- Administration might cover the accounting department as well as legal fees, office supplies, bad debts, and education, among other things.
- Your fixed expenses will include insurance, depreciation, rents or leases, interest on loans, and taxes.

COSTS AND EXPENSES HIGHLIGHTS

Inventory

We do a full liquor inventory every week and compare it to our sales. Your liquor is one of the easiest products to lose and the hardest to track. Tracking complimentary drinks and spillage is as important as counting your safe at the end of the day.

Many drinks have partial shots of liquors such as a Long Island Iced Tea. Liquor companies saw the need for tracking inventory and came out with a pre-mix of vodka, rum, and gin for LIITs, but every day a bartender creates a new "Hot" drink that uses a variety of liquors.

You will also have other items like paper goods and glassware. If your staff is throwing silverware into the trash or taking bar towels home to clean their car, your dry goods budget will take a hit. Keeping inventory on these items will tell you where the losses are coming from and help you stop the bleeding.

We count juices, sodas, boutique items, and dry goods once a month. When the bookkeeper does the financials at the end of the month, the owners/investors can see the value of the assets on hand. Too much on hand, and there will be no money to distribute to your owners/investors. Too little on hand, and you can't sell what you don't have.

Entertainer Lease Fees

We employ a computer-based entertainment tracking system. When an entertainer pays her rental fee, the manager enters it into the computer. At the end of the day, the entertainer checks out and exchanges her ones for larger bills.

The system can tell us how many hours she worked, how many times she was on stage, how many private dances she performed, and if she was out of the rotation. This helps us monitor whether she is making money and keeps our managers and DJs from putting entertainment fees in their pockets.

Payroll

When budgeting for payroll, remember the employer matches the employee's Social Security withholding. You will also have unemployment insurance and Workers Comp payments based on the number of people you employ.

Fine-tuning your schedules will always be a challenge. A week with a tradeshow in town can mean double the business or nothing at all. Schedule for the crowd you want. If a guest comes in and can't get a drink, he won't be back, or he'll tell his friends your service is bad. You are in the business of pretty girls, you can't schedule the entertainers if they are contracted, but you can fill the room with pretty waitresses.

Most new owners don't understand the importance of paying for good managers. Lack of good management is the most frequent problem suffered by bars and nightclubs. A team of managers who continuously train the support staff will attract the kind of employees and guests you want. If your club is correctly run, your bar staff will make enough in tips to attract quality servers and, more importantly, quality entertainers.

Legal

Get a lawyer from the very beginning to help you navigate the operating agreement and contracts with your partners. It is also helpful to have a lawyer look over, if not help you finalize, the lease agreement if you don't own the property.

Keeping a good lawyer on retainer is a wise investment. State liquor boards often have a say in what style of entertainment is allowed in clubs that serves alcohol. Beyond that, you will be facing a myriad of rules and regulations regarding proximity to schools, churches, other bars, and residential housing. Hire someone or several people who understand employment laws, tax laws, and health codes. All of these will affect how you run your business.

We are not lawyers and can only tell you what we have done. You need to seek out legal counsel from the beginning. Shotgun Willie's is a Limited Liability Company or LLC to help protect the owners and our partners from personal lawsuits. We never know where the next lawsuit will come from. In today's society, lawyers are permitted to run ads on television, convincing everyone they have the right to sue for everything. It's one thing to follow the myriad of employment laws; it's another to prove you have followed all the laws. And that is going to cost you a ton of money.

Insurances

Even before the first employee is hired, a business is at risk, making it important to have the right insurance in place. One lawsuit or catastrophic event could be enough to wipe out a small business before it even has a chance to get off the ground. The amount, types, and cost of insurances will depend greatly on your location and gross sales. Get a lawyer and savvy insurance broker.

Some of the Insurances you may need include:
General Liability Insurance Professional liability insurance, also known as errors and omissions (E&O) insurance, covers a business against negligence claims due to harm that results from mistakes or failure to perform. Make sure your liability insurance covers you if an employee gets into an altercation. Many policies don't cover this. We do everything in our power to prevent fights, but we deal with humans and alcohol. A good average policy is at least $2 million in blanket coverage.
Workers Compensation Covers medical treatment, disability, and death benefits in the event an employee is injured or dies because of his work with that business. Slip-and-fall injuries or medical conditions such as carpal tunnel syndrome could result in a pricey claim.
Property insurance Whether a business owns or leases its space, property insurance is necessary. This insurance covers equipment, signage, inventory, and furniture in the event of a fire, storm, or theft.
Business Interruption or Catastrophic You might suffer a major monetary loss due to a lawsuit or catastrophic event.

Check with your insurance broker to find out what forms of insurance are advised for restaurants, bars, and nightclubs and put those plans in place as soon as possible.

Licenses and Fees

You're going to need several state licenses, possibly separate licenses for cigars, entertainment, food, beer, wine, and liquor. These include but aren't limited to sales tax licenses.

Taxes

While doing business, your club will owe some level of corporate, sales, and payroll (employer) taxes. There will be federal and state and local taxes as well. Keeping good records will save you in an audit. Every receipt, every check, every invoice needs to be filed away and kept in a safe place. Even if you are only running a small club, accounting is important. The good news is, your accountants and bookkeepers don't have to be personable, only accurate.

Capital Improvements

If possible, work directly with the landlord if you don't own the building. You may need to make structural changes to the building, improvements like carpeting and plumbing for bars, so having a good rapport with the landlord is important. The cost of repairing or improving property used in your trade or business is usually a deductible or capital expense. A good accountant can be invaluable when working out the tax details of assets and capital improvements.

Cleaning, Maintenance, and Repairs

In this business, you will be spending a lot of money keeping the place in good condition. Some of these costs are tax-deductible. See your accountant for details. Similar to your payroll and inventory, this is an important part of your budget. Keep in mind, if you do *Mashed Potato Wrestling* the night before Thanksgiving, you're going to need a crew (on holiday pay) to come in and clean it up.

Marketing and Advertising

Marketing expenses can include formal advertising expenses, as well as the cost of meals and entertainment incurred while promoting the business. Some other marketing expense deductions may include business cards, local sponsorships, seminars, trade shows, and modest business gifts. In most cases, business-related meals and entertainment expenses for entertaining a client, customer, or employee may also be considered.

Advertising Expense refers to the specific cost incurred in promoting a business via newspapers and magazines, television, radio, the internet, billboards, flyers, and others.

Fixed costs vs. Flexible Costs

Some costs will be the same if you have ten guests or two hundred. Accountant fees, lawyer retainers, building leases, phone service, security services, and business licenses come to mind.

Beyond that, there will be costs that vary depending on how much business you do. Payroll, liquor, and dry goods are costs that will increase as you grow. Once you've set your budget, you need to monitor those items to see that they only rise at the rate of business growth.

If inflation has raised your costs on these items, you will need to raise your prices to get your business back on track. A dollar an hour raise to an employee will cost you about $1.50 in total costs.

APPENDICES

APPENDIX I – SAMPLE ACCOUNTING FORMS
Instructions and documents used daily to track cash, credit cards, and more.

APPENDIX II – POLICY HANDBOOK SAMPLE

APPENDIX III – NEW HIRE PACKET SAMPLE

APPENDIX IV – TRAINING MANUAL SAMPLE

Sample Accounting Forms

The information provided is not to be construed as legal or accounting advice but merely an indication of the laws and practices needed to run a business of this type. Please consult your attorney, accountant, and insurance broker for details and questions.

Appendix I Contents

BANK RECONCILIATION FORM

This sample Bank Reconciliation form allows you to track the beginning banks given to your staff and banks returned at the end of the shift. This, combined with the Safe Reconciliation form, allows you to see where all your cash is at any given time.

BANK RECONCILIATION 800

CLUB _______________ DAY _________________ DATE _________________

AM MANAGER _______________

Issued	Employee	Bank Amount	Intl	Returned Anount
Bar 1	__________	__________	______	__________
Bar 2	__________	__________	______	__________
Bar 3	__________	__________	______	__________
Bar 4	__________	__________	______	__________
Bar 5	__________	__________	______	__________
Bar 6	__________	__________	______	__________
Cashier	__________	__________	______	__________
Door 1	__________	__________	______	__________
Door 2	__________	__________	______	__________
Door 3	__________	__________	______	__________

TOTAL BANKS ISSUED _________________

AMOUNT RETURNED _________________

OWED TO SAFE ----- AMOUNT SHORT _________________

PM MANAGER _______________

Issued	Employee	Bank Amount	Intl	Returned Anount
Bar 1	__________	__________	______	__________
Bar 2	__________	__________	______	__________
Bar 3	__________	__________	______	__________
Bar 4	__________	__________	______	__________
Bar 5	__________	__________	______	__________
Bar 6	__________	__________	______	__________
Cashier	__________	__________	______	__________
Door 1	__________	__________	______	__________
Door 2	__________	__________	______	__________
Door 3	__________	__________	______	__________

TOTAL BANK ISSUED _________________

AMOUNT RETURNED _________________

OWED TO SAFE ----- AMOUNT SHORT _________________

SINGLE BARREL CONSULTING, LLC | 800|

SAFE RECONCILIATION FORM

This form helps you track cash in and out of your main safe, including petty cash slips. At the beginning and the end of each shift, the manager should balance/verify his safe before passing it to the next manager. We open each day with only quarters, ones, and fives. The amount you will need each day will depend on your business. For instance: if your beginning safe is $20,000, you would probably have $500 in quarters, $1,500 in fives, and $18,000 in ones. **Note**: the day shift has a line for an outstanding change order should monies be on order from your banking facility.

Safe Reconciliation 803

DAY ____________   DATE ____________

MANAGER ____________   MANAGER ____________

Opening Count		Mid Day Count	
Quarers	$	Quarers	$
Ones	$	Ones	$
Twos	$	Twos	$
Fives	$	Fives	$
Tens	$	Tens	$
Twenties	$	Twenties	$
Fifties	$	Fifties	$
Hundreds	$	Hundreds	$
Checks	$	Checks	
Paidouts	$	Paidouts	
Total Safe	$	Total Safe	$
Banks Issued	$	Banks Issued	$
Change Order	$	Change Order	$
TOTAL HOUSE	$	TOTAL HOUSE	$
Over/Short	$	Over/Short	$

MANAGER ____________

Closing Count			
Quarers	$		
Ones	$		
Twos	$	Total Safe	$
Fives	$	Banks Owed	$
Tens	$	TOTAL HOUSE	$
Twenties	$		
Fifties	$	Over/Short	$
Hundreds	$		
Checks	$		
Paidouts	$		
Total Safe	$		

SINGLE BARREL CONSULTING, LLC GLENDALE, CO

ENTERTAINMENT DOLLARS TRACKING

Along with your cash is the issue of your Entertainment Dollars. The following form helps you track which boxes of Entertainment Dollars are issued. At the beginning of the day, the accounting office issues $10,000 in Entertainment Dollars to the opening manager. Ten numbered boxes with $1,000 in each numbered box. At the end of the shift, the bartender returns any unsold Dollars and a signed reciept from the sale of any missing Dollars. The Day manager balances the Entertainment Dollars and passes the balance to the night manager.

ENTERTAINMENT DOLLAR TRACKING

DAY _______________ DATE _____________ Bookkeeper _______________

DGD ISSUED _______________ Manager Verified _______________

AM Sold $ _______ boxes Issued _______ Bartender _______ Returned _______

AM Sold $ _______ boxes Issued _______ Bartender _______ Returned _______

Balance to PM $ _______ Manager Verified _______________

AM Sold $ _______ boxes Issued _______ Bartender _______ Returned _______

AM Sold $ _______ boxes Issued _______ Bartender _______ Returned _______

AM Sold $ _______ boxes Issued _______ Bartender _______ Returned _______

AM Sold $ _______ boxes Issued _______ Bartender _______ Returned _______

AM Sold $ _______ boxes Issued _______ Bartender _______ Returned _______

AM Sold $ _______ boxes Issued _______ Bartender _______ Returned _______

Total DGDs Sold $ _______ Manager Verified Amount Returned _______________

DGD ISSUED $ _______

Additional Bump $ _______

Redeemed $ _______

Minus DGDs Sold $ _______

Total returned $ _______

TAXI Bank Issued	_______
TAXI Rides	_______
TAXI Incentives	_______
Total Returned	_______
VALET	

Actual returned $ _______ Bookkeeper _______________

SINGLE BARREL CONSULTING, LLC GLENDALE, CO   ETD Tracking 807

We also issue money to out valet to cover the cost of providing a safe ride home for intoxicated guests and incentives for cab drivers to bring us guests. **Note:** Money paid to cab drivers for incentives must be tracked and you must have a W-9 for each one.

BARTENDER CHECKOUT FORM

We have all the waitresses close their credit cards and cash tabs through the bartender as a double-check and to limit the number of check-outs at the end of the night. You may choose to do them separately. Once you have the cash counted, add the credit cards and Entertainer Dollars used to purchase drinks or food. Because of the fee to use Entertainment Dollars, this is rare. Subtract the amount due from your register tape and fill in the over or short.

BARTENDER CHECKOUT

BARTENDER ________________   DATE ________________

MANAGER ________________   SHIFT ________________

ONES __________   Total Cash in __________
Credit Cards __________
FIVES __________   Et Dollars in __________

TENS __________   TOTAL IN __________
Less TAPE
TWENTIES __________   OVER\SHORT __________

FIFTIES __________

HUNDREDS __________   ETD BOX #s __________

COINS __________   ETD Amount $ __________
(Issued)
Total Cash in __________   ETD SOLD $ __________
move to top line column two
RETURNED __________
(Not Sold)

OVER\SHORT __________

SIGNATURE ______________________

SBC Bar Checkout 806

The lower box is to account for the Entertainment Dollars sold to be sure the proper amount of Dollars are returned. Your door check out will be the same as your bar check out minus the Entertainment Dollars issued unless you choose to have your Door Host sell Entertainment Dollars.

MANAGER CHECKOUT FORM

The manager will collect the lease fees from the entertainers. Shortly before the end of his shift he should turn in his checkout slip with the cash. On this slip there is a place to denote entertainers who did not pay fees but worked.

MANAGER CHECKOUT

MANAGER _______	**DATE** _______	
CASHIER _______	**SHIFT** _______	

ONES _______	**PROMOTIONS (free shifts)**	
	Type	Entertainer
FIVES _______	_______	
TENS _______	_______	
TWENTIES _______	_______	
FIFTIES _______	_______	
HUNDREDS _______	_______	
COINS _______	_______	
ET DOLLARS _______	_______	
TOTAL IN _______	_______	

	AUDITIONS (free shifts)	
LEASE FEES _______	_______	
OFF LIST FEES _______	_______	
TOTAL DUE _______	_______	
TOTAL IN _______		
OVER\SHORT _______	_______	

SIGNATURE _______________________

SBC Manager Checkout 802

CASHIER CHECKOUT FORM

Entertainers' are assigned a dedicated Cashier (affectionately known as *Miss Kitty)* who is responsible for:

- exchanging Entertainment Dollars or ones for larger denominations of cash
- overseeing the dance area to help keep the girls safe
- collecting the admission fee for dances
- tracking the Entertainers who come out of rotation
- clocking the Entertainers out at the end of the night
- giving the Entertainers a voucher to be escorted to their car by the valet

CASHIER CHECKOUT

CASHIER ___________   DATE _______ DAY ___________

MANAGER ___________   TOTAL BANK ISSUED ___________
                      AMOUNT RETURNED ___________
                      AMOUNT SHORT ___________
                      (Owed to safe)

# SOLD	ITEM	AMOUNT DUE		CASH TURNED IN
______	OFF LIST	$ ______	Ones	$ ______
______	AM DANCES	$ ______	Twos	$ ______
______	PM DANCES	$ ______	Fives	$ ______
______	AM FEES	$ ______	Tens	$ ______
______	PM FEES	$ ______	Twenties	$ ______
______	RETAIL	$ ______	Fifties	$ ______
______	ADMISSIONS	$ ______	Hundreds	$ ______
______	B-PARTIES	$ ______	Coins	$ ______

SALES =   TOTAL DUE $ ______   Total Cash In $ ______

MANAGER CHECK OUTS		Other Receipts	
		DGD Tips	$ ______
MANAGER	______	Credit Card	$ ______
AM FEES	$ ______	B-Parties	$ ______
AM DROP	$ ______		
over/short	$ ______	TOTAL CASH	
		AND RECEIPTS	$ ______
MANAGER	______	Less Owe to safe	$ ______
PM FEES	$ ______	TOTAL IN	$ ______
PM DROP	$ ______	AMOUNT DUE	$ ______
over/short	$ ______		
		OVER/SHORT	$ ______
TOTAL DAY			
over/short	$ ______		

SINGLE BARREL CONSULTING, LLC GLENDALE, CO   Cashier Checkout 801

All checkouts have cash separated from credit cards to help the accounting department with tracking.

Managers should also turn in their checkout forms to *Miss Kitty personnel.*

CHANGE ORDER REQUEST FORM

On the form below, you can see all the large bills are listed and the request for smaller bills. Ones, fives, and quarters are returned to the safe before we place an order for change from the bank. On your Safe Reconciliation sheet you will find a line to enter this total to balance your safe.

CHANGE ORDER REQUEST

MANAGER _______________   DATE _______________________

No. of Bills	Denominations	Amount
300	Hundreds	$3,000.00
100	Fifties	$5,000.00
460	Twenties	$9,200.00
450	Ten	$4,500.00
	Fives	
	Ones	
	Quarters	
	Total	$21,700.00

CHANGE NEEDED

No. of Bills	Denominations	Amount
	Hundreds	
	Fifties	
	Twenties	
	Ten	
	Fives	$1,500.00
	Ones	$20,000.00
	Quarters	$200.00
	Total	$21,700.00

SINGLE BARREL CONSULTING, LLC GLENDALE, CO   SBC CHANGE ORDER 808

DAILY AM MANAGER LOG

Daily **AM** Manager Log

Day: _______________ Date: _______________ Manager/s: _________________________________

Gross: _______________ ⇧ ⇩ _______________

Guests _______ ⇧ ⇩ _______ D/A: _______________ Guest List#_________ Showed:_________

ETS: 11-7: _______ 2-8: _______ 4-10: _______ Cigar Sales: _______ Retail Sales: _______

Daily Promotional Event: ____

Overview:

Which customer spent the most money? What was his/her name? What did they drink and which ETs did they sit with? How much did they spend?

Which support staff member brought in the most people? _________________________________

What parties were booked today? Who booked them? What is the occasion?

Social Media ☐   Music:____

HR Paperwork ☐   Discipline:____

Staff Dress-up ☐   Rockstar Staff:____

Shadow Box ☐   Rockstar ET's:____

Fire Pole ☐   New ET's:____

Workshop ☐   Show Stoppers ☐

White Board: " ____

____

____ "

DAILY MID MANAGER LOG

Daily **MID** Manager Log

Day: _______________ Date: _______________ Manager/s: _______________________________________

Gross: _____________________ ⬆ ⬇ _______________

Guests _______ ⬆ ⬇ _______ D/A: _____________ Guest List#__________ Showed:__________

ETS: 4-10: _______ 7: _______ Cigar Sales: ________ Retail Sales: ________

Daily Promotional Event: ____

Overview:

Which customer spent the most money? What was his/her name? What did they drink and which ETs did they sit with? How much did they spend?

Which support staff member brought in the most people?____

What parties were booked today? Who booked them? What is the occasion?

Social Media ☐   Music:____

HR Paperwork ☐   Discipline:____

Staff Dress-up ☐   Rockstar Staff:____

Shadow Box ☐   Rockstar ET's:____

Fire Pole ☐   New ET's:____

Workshop ☐   Show Stoppers ☐

DAILY PM MANAGER LOG

<table>
<tr><td colspan="2">

Daily **PM** Manager Log

Day: _____________ Date: _____________

Manager/s: ___________________________________

Gross: ___________________ ⬆ ⬇ _____________

Day: _____________ ⬆ ⬇ _____________

Week: ___________________ ⬆ ⬇ _____________

Guests __________ ⬆ ⬇ _______ D/A: _________

ETS: 8: _______ 9: _______ 10: _______

Off List: _________ Table Dance: _________

</td><td>

TBAR

Gross $: _________________

Bartender: _____________

Door Host: _____________

Monitor: _______________

</td></tr>
</table>

Guest List#__________ Showed:__________

Cigar Sales: __________ Retail Sales:________

Daily Promotional Event: _______________________________________

Out of house Promotions: _______________________________________

Overview:

Which customer spent the most money? What was his/her name? What did they drink and which ETs did they sit with? How much did they spend?

Limos and Busses: What were the driver's names? Did you buy them a meal? Did you do anything special for them?

What parties were booked today? Who booked them? What is the occasion?

Social Media ☐   Music:____

HR Paperwork ☐   Discipline:_______________________________________

Staff Dress-up ☐   Rockstar Staff:___________________________________

Shadow Box ☐   Rockstar ET's:____________________________________

Fire Pole ☐   New ET's:____

Workshop ☐   Show Stoppers ☐

DAILY SALES FORM

DAILY SALES | 901

Daily Sales

Bookkeeper

Date: ___________ Day: ___________

Sales	Acct#	dr	cr
Food	4310		
Liquor	4010		
Wine	4110		
Bottle Beer	4210		
Draft Beer	4220		
Retail	4405		
Cigars	4320		
Tax 8.0%	2250		
Door Admissions	4410		
Tax 3.5%	2250		
$5 Table Dance Admit Fee	4415		
Tax 3.5%	2250		
DGD Sold	4545		
DGD Surcharge	4540		
Off list Fees	4510		
ET License Fees	5885		
Change Order Check	1010		
Cigarettes	4530		
Gift Cards	1835		
Donations	1520		
Total		$ -	$ -

Total Cash/Checks In $ ___________
Safe (over)/ Short $ ___________
Banks Due Back $ ___________
Paid Outs $ ___________
TOTAL DEPOSIT $ ___________

Revenue	Acct#	dr	cr
Bar Bank Acct-4821	1055		
MCVS/AMEX/Discover	1110		
Comp Food	8560		
Taxis paid out	7250		
Over/Short	8080		
DGD Redeemed Tips	4550		
DGD Redeemed Gift Certifica	4560		
Total		$ -	$ -
Variance			$ -

Check Outs Over/Short $ ___________
Credit Cards Over/Short $ ___________
Safe Over/Short $ ___________
Paid Outs Rounding $ ___________
TOTAL Over/Short $ ___________

INCIDENT WITNESS REPORT

INCIDENT REPORT 901

INCIDENT WITNESS REPORT

Type of Incident ___________ Date: _________ Day: __________ Time __________

Police Involved Yes ___ NO ___ Case # _________ Officer _________ Officer __________

Name of Business _______________________ Location _______________________

Address _______________________

City _______________ State / Zip

Business Phone _______________________ Manager on Duty _______________________

Name of Witness _______________________

Last Name   First Name   Occupation   Date of Birth

Witness Address _______________________

City   State / Zip

I, _______________________ , do hearby make the following statement concerning the incident.

Yo, _______________________ , hago la siguente declaracion volintariamente en el incidente que pasc

____

____

____

____

____

____

____

____

____

____

Use more sheets if necessary.
Please sign your name at the bottom of this sheet and place your initials at the end of your statement.
I affirm that the information contained herein is true and correct
Yo affirmo que la informacion en este declaracion es la verded y esta correcto.

X ____

SINGLE BARREL CONDULTING, LLC

Single Barrel Consulting, LLC

Policy Handbook

Table of Contents

I. <u>SINGLE BARREL CONSULTING, LLC</u> HISTORY

<u>Single Barrel Consulting, LLC</u>, was established in 2017. The founding members are Deborah Matthews, owner, and Michele Poague, 35-year-plus manager, of Shotgun Willies, known internationally as one of the country's leading entertainment establishments.

II. MISSION STATEMENT

It is our goal to create the most exceptional experience anywhere on the planet. By treating every person who comes through our doors, calls on our phone, or works with us as a unique individual, we recognize the "spark" of individuality in ourselves as well as in others. We strive to communicate this in an honest and sincere by offering the finest adult products and entertainment available.

FIVE STAR SERVICE. We strive for professionalism and teamwork. To reach our goal, we follow these guidelines. Keep in mind that not any single point is more important than another; it is the combination that produces Five Star Service.

ATTITUDE AND APPEARANCE. Attitude and appearance go hand-in-hand. If you look good, you feel good and if you feel good, you look good. If you act like you're having fun, those around you will have fun. There is no room on the set for personal problems. Not only does it affect your performance, it affects those around you. Our guests notice small things like hair and fingernails. We understand that it is difficult to be "perfect" every day, but we expect you to do the very best you can.

KNOWLEDGE. Know your duties and responsibilities thoroughly. Know procedures and promotions. If there is something you don't know or understand, ASK. The worst thing you can say to a guest is: "I don't know." Saying "I don't know" suggests you don't care. It is far better to say: "I'll find out," or "I'll check on that for you."

SERVICE. We cannot stress the "importance of smiling" enough. One smile will do what a thousand words cannot. We cater to our guests. We do the extra little things to make them feel special. "Every Guest is Entitled to the Same Service."

BUILD A CLIENTELE. A regular clientele will increase your tips. Learn the art of small talk. Learn to be witty without being catty. Make sure every guest feels welcome and special. We refer to our audience as our "guest" rather than "customer" – we expect them to be treated as such. Learn the names of the guests and make sure they know yours. They will ask for you the next time they come in.

APPRECIATION. It is because of our audience that we have a business. This includes the guest who cannot afford a large tip as well as the guest who can. Always thank a guest for a tip no matter what the amount. Let them know you are glad they are here. When they leave, thank them for coming and invite them back. A dollar one day is worth less than a quarter five days a week.

III. OVERVIEW

This Employee Handbook (the "Handbook") has been developed to provide general guidelines about our Company policies and procedures for employees. It is a guide to assist you in becoming familiar with some of the privileges and obligations of your employment, including Company policy of voluntary at-will employment. None of the policies or guidelines in the Handbook are intended to give rise to contractual rights or obligations, or to be construed as a guarantee of employment for any specific period of time, or any specific type of work. Additionally, apart from the voluntary at-will employment policy, these guidelines are subject to modification, amendment or revocation by Single Barrel Consulting, LLC at any time, without advance notice.

The personnel policies of Single Barrel Consulting, LLC are established by the Board of Directors, which has delegated authority and responsibility for their administration to Deborah Matthews Dunafon and Michele Poague, the Executive Director and Chief Executive Officer. The Executive Director or Chief Executive Officer may, in turn, delegate authority for administering specific policies. Employees are encouraged to consult his or her immediate supervisor for additional information regarding the policies, procedures, and privileges described in this Handbook. Questions about personnel matters also may be reviewed with Deborah Matthews Dunafon, or Michele Poague.

Single Barrel Consulting, LLC will provide everyone a copy of this Handbook upon employment. All employees are expected to abide by it. The highest standards of personal and professional ethics and behavior are expected of all Single Barrel Consulting, LLC employees. Further, Single Barrel Consulting, LLC expects each employee to display good judgment, diplomacy and courtesy in their professional relationships with members of Single Barrel Consulting, LLC' Board of Directors, committees, membership, staff, and the general public.

IV. VOLUNTARY AT-WILL EMPLOYMENT

Unless an employee has a written employment agreement with Single Barrel Consulting, LLC, which provides differently, all employment at Single Barrel Consulting, LLC is "at-will."

"At-will" means that employees:

- can be terminated from employment with Single Barrel Consulting, LLC, with or without cause,
- are free to leave the employment of Single Barrel Consulting, LLC, with or without cause.

Any representation by any Single Barrel Consulting, LLC' officer or employee contrary to this policy is not binding upon Single Barrel Consulting, LLC unless it is in writing and is signed by the Executive Director or Chief Executive Officer.

V. ARBITRATION OF DISPUTES

Because of the delay and expense involved in litigation before state or federal courts or federal agencies, <u>Single Barrel Consulting, LLC</u> and its employees understand and agree that any claim or dispute arising out of or relating to recruitment, hiring, employment or termination from employment with <u>Single Barrel Consulting, LLC</u> shall be subject to final and binding arbitration, pursuant to the Federal Arbitration Act 9,U.S.C -1 et seq. and the Colorado Arbitration Act.

Arbitration is conducted in Denver, Colorado.

Claims which must be arbitrated under this agreement include but are not limited to:
- any and all claims on common law, whether in tort or contract;
- any employment discrimination, harassment, or retaliation claims based on federal or state law, including claims based upon Title VII, The Americans with Disabilities Act, and The Age Discrimination in Employment Act;
- claims for violation of the Family Medical Leave Act;
- claims for violation of the Fair Labor Standards Act;
- claims for violation of public policy or for whistleblowing;
- any claim based on any state or federal statute;
- any claim based on any state or federal constitutional provision; and
- any amendments or modifications to such laws.

However, any claim by the Employee for unemployment or workers' compensation benefits is not subject to mandatory arbitration under this agreement.

The agreement to arbitrate any claim or dispute arising out of or relating to an employee's recruitment, hiring, employment or termination from employment with <u>Single Barrel Consulting, LLC</u> shall include any and all claims brought against any agent, insurer, co-employee, supervisor, manager, office, owner, director, or shareholder of <u>Single Barrel Consulting, LLC</u> present, future or former, if said claim or dispute relates to or arises out of or relating to my recruitment, hiring, employment or termination from employment with <u>Single Barrel Consulting, LLC</u>. Consolidation of separate arbitration proceedings is prohibited.

Arbitration may be initiated by either party providing the other party with a written notice of claim which describes the nature of the dispute and a demand for arbitration. This notice must be given by certified or registered mail, return receipt requested and obtained, or by service authorized for commencement of a civil action.

The arbitration of any dispute under this Agreement shall be conducted pursuant to the then existing arbitration rules and procedure of Dispute Prevention and Resolution, Inc. (DPR) The Parties agree to use the Arbitrator selection procedures set forth by the DPR.

This Agreement regarding arbitration of disputes between the employee and <u>Single Barrel Consulting, LLC</u> may only be modified by a writing that is signed by both the employee and the Executive Director of <u>Single Barrel Consulting, LLC</u>.

Single Barrel Consulting, LLC will pay reasonable costs of arbitration including filing fees and arbitrator expenses. Each party shall his/her/its own attorney's fees and costs, if any. However, the arbitrator may, at his/her discretion, permit the prevailing party to recover fees and costs to the extent permitted by applicable law. Neither party, however, forgoes and substantive rights or remedies as provided by law.

THE EMPLOYEE AGREES TO KEEP ALL PROCEEDINGS AND MATTERS SUBJECT TO THIS AGREEMENT COMPLETELY CONFIDENTIAL. HOWEVER, THE EMPLOYEE UNDERSTANDS THAT HE/SHE HAS THE RIGHT TO RETAIN COUNSEL OF HIS/HER CHOICE IF DESIRED.

THE EMPLOYEE UNDERSTANDS THAT BY SIGNING THIS AGREEMENT, HE/SHE RELINQUISHES THE RIGHT TO A TRAIL BY A JUDGE, JURY, OR ADMINISTRATIVE AGENCY, OF ANY CLAIM OR DISPUTE RELATING TO OR ARISING OUT OF HIS/HER RECRUITMENT, HIRING, EMPLOYMENT OR TERMINATION WITH SINGLE BARREL CONSULTING, LLC.

ENTIRE AGREEMENT. The employee acknowledges and agrees that this Agreement contains the entire agreement and understanding between the employee and Single Barrel Consulting, LLC. This agreement supersedes all other agreements, whether oral or in writing, relating to the subject matter herein.

SEVERABILITY OF PROVISION. The parties intend that this agreement be enforceable to the fullest extent permitted by law. Should any term or provision of this Agreement be determined to be illegal, void, or invalid, such terms shall be considered severed or modified to conform to the law, and the remaining terms and provisions of this agreement shall continue in full force and effect

MISCELLANEOUS. This agreement shall be binding and pass to the benefit of the successors and assigns of Single Barrel Consulting, LLC. This Agreement survives and extends beyond my termination of employment. Waiver by the company of any particular breach of this Agreement by the employee shall not be deemed a waiver by Single Barrel Consulting, LLC of any of my promises or obligations herein, or of any subsequent breach by the employee.

VI. EQUAL EMPLOYMENT OPPORTUNITY

Single Barrel Consulting, LLC shall follow the spirit and intent of all federal, state and local employment law. Single Barrel Consulting, LLC is committed to equal employment opportunity. To that end, the Board of Directors or management of Single Barrel Consulting, LLC will not discriminate against any employee or applicant in a manner that violates the law. Single Barrel Consulting, LLC is committed to providing equal opportunity for all employees and applicants without regard to race, color, religion, national origin, sex, age, marital status, sexual orientation, disability, political affiliation, personal appearance, family responsibilities, matriculation or any other characteristic protected under federal, state or local law. Each person is evaluated on the basis of personal skill and merit. Single Barrel Consulting, LLC' policy regarding equal employment opportunity applies to all aspects of employment, including recruitment, hiring, job assignments, promotions, working conditions, scheduling, benefits, wage and salary administration, disciplinary action, termination, and social, educational and recreational programs. The Executive Director shall act as the responsible agent in the full implementation of the Equal Employment Opportunity policy.

Single Barrel Consulting, LLC will not tolerate any form of unlawful discrimination. All employees are expected to cooperate fully in implementing this policy. In particular, any employee who believes that any other employee of Single Barrel Consulting, LLC may have violated the Equal Employment Opportunity Policy should report the possible violation to the Human Resources Department.

If Single Barrel Consulting, LLC determines that a violation of this policy has occurred, it will take appropriate disciplinary action against the offending party, which can include counseling, warnings, suspensions, and termination. Employees who report, in good faith, violations of this policy and employees who cooperate with investigations into alleged violations of this policy will not be subject to retaliation. Upon completion of the investigation, Single Barrel Consulting, LLC will inform the employee who made the complaint of the results of the investigation.

Single Barrel Consulting, LLC is also committed to complying fully with applicable disability discrimination laws, and ensuring that equal opportunity in employment exists at Single Barrel Consulting, LLC for qualified persons with disabilities. All employment practices and activities are conducted on a non-discriminatory basis. Reasonable accommodations will be available to all qualified disabled employees, upon request, so long as the potential accommodation does not create an undue hardship on Single Barrel Consulting, LLC. Employees who believe that they may require an accommodation should discuss these needs with the Human Resources Department.

VII. POLICY AGAINST WORKPLACE HARASSMENT

Single Barrel Consulting, LLC is committed to providing a work environment for all employees that is free from sexual harassment and other types of discriminatory harassment. Employees are expected to conduct themselves in a professional manner and to show respect for their co-workers.

Single Barrel Consulting, LLC' commitment begins with the recognition and acknowledgment that sexual harassment and other types of discriminatory harassment are, of course, unlawful. To reinforce this commitment, Single Barrel Consulting, LLC has developed a policy against harassment and a reporting procedure for employees who have been subjected to or witnessed harassment. This policy applies to all work-related settings and activities, whether inside or outside the workplace, and includes business trips and business-related social events. Single Barrel Consulting, LLC' property (e.g. telephones, copy machines, facsimile machines, computers, and computer applications such as e-mail and Internet access) may not be used to engage in conduct that violates this policy. Single Barrel Consulting, LLC' policy against harassment covers employees and other individuals who have a relationship with Single Barrel Consulting, LLC which enables Single Barrel Consulting, LLC to exercise some control over the individual's conduct in places and activities that relate to Single Barrel Consulting, LLC' work (e.g. directors, officers, contractors, vendors, volunteers, etc.).

PROHIBITION OF SEXUAL HARASSMENT: <u>Single Barrel Consulting, LLC</u>' policy against sexual harassment prohibits sexual advances or requests for sexual favors or other physical or verbal conduct of a sexual nature, when: (1) submission to such conduct is made an express or implicit condition of employment; (2) submission to or rejection of such conduct is used as a basis for employment decisions affecting the individual who submits to or rejects such conduct; or (3) such conduct has the purpose or effect of unreasonably interfering with an employee's work performance or creating an intimidating, hostile, humiliating, or offensive working environment.

While it is not possible to list all of the circumstances which would constitute sexual harassment, the following are some examples: (1) unwelcome sexual advances -- whether they involve physical touching or not; (2) requests for sexual favors in exchange for actual or promised job benefits such as favorable reviews, salary increases, promotions, increased benefits, or continued employment; or (3) coerced sexual acts.

<u>Single Barrel Consulting, LLC</u> is an adult entertainment establishment that provides entertainment to our guests that is sexual in nature. Including but not limited to: (1) use of sexual epithets, jokes, written or oral references to sexual conduct, gossip regarding one's sex life; (2) sexually oriented comment on an individual's body, comment about an individual's sexual activity, deficiencies, or prowess; (3) displaying sexually suggestive objects, pictures, cartoons; (4) unwelcome leering, whistling, deliberate brushing against the body in a suggestive manner; (5) sexual gestures or sexually suggestive comments; (6) inquiries into one's sexual experiences; or (7) discussion of one's sexual activities.

We also recognize that, depending on the circumstances, the following conduct may constitute sexual harassment: (1) use of sexual epithets, jokes, written or oral references to sexual conduct, gossip regarding one's sex life; (2) sexually oriented comment on an individual's body, comment about an individual's sexual activity, deficiencies, or prowess; (3) displaying sexually suggestive objects, pictures, cartoons; (4) unwelcome leering, whistling, deliberate brushing against the body in a suggestive manner; (5) sexual gestures or sexually suggestive comments; (6) inquiries into one's sexual experiences; or (7) discussion of one's sexual activities.

While such behavior, depending on the circumstances, may not be severe or pervasive enough to create a sexually hostile work environment, it can nonetheless make co-workers uncomfortable. It is the desire of <u>Single Barrel Consulting, LLC</u> to be a fun working environment without distressing any employee. If you have any questions regarding this policy, please contact the Human Resources Department.

It is also unlawful and expressly against Company policy to retaliate against an employee for filing a complaint of sexual harassment or for cooperating with an investigation of a complaint of sexual harassment.

Prohibition of Other Types of Discriminatory Harassment: It is also against Company policy to engage in verbal or physical conduct that denigrates or shows hostility or aversion toward an individual because of his or her race, color, gender, religion, sexual orientation, age, national origin, disability, or other protected category (or that of the individual's relatives, friends, or associates) that: (1) has the purpose or effect of creating an intimidating, hostile, humiliating, or offensive working environment; (2) has the purpose or effect of unreasonably interfering with an individual's work performance; or (3) otherwise adversely affects an individual's employment opportunities.

Depending on the circumstances, the following conduct may constitute discriminatory harassment: (1) epithets, slurs, negative stereotyping, jokes, or threatening, intimidating, or hostile acts that relate to race, color, gender, religion, sexual orientation, age, national origin, or disability; and (2) written or graphic material that denigrates or shows hostility toward an individual or group because of race, color, gender, religion, sexual orientation, age, national origin, or disability and that is circulated in the workplace, or placed anywhere on Single Barrel Consulting, LLC' premises such as on an employee's desk or workspace or on Single Barrel Consulting, LLC' equipment or bulletin boards. Other conduct may also constitute discriminatory harassment if it falls within the definition of discriminatory harassment set forth above.

It is also against Company policy to retaliate against an employee for filing a complaint of discriminatory harassment or for cooperating in an investigation of a complaint of discriminatory harassment.

Reporting of Harassment: If you believe that you have experienced or witnessed sexual harassment or other discriminatory harassment by any employee of Single Barrel Consulting, LLC, you should report the incident immediately to your supervisor or to the Human Resources Department. Possible harassment by others with whom Single Barrel Consulting, LLC has a business relationship, including customers and vendors, should also be reported as soon as possible so that appropriate action can be taken.

Single Barrel Consulting, LLC will promptly and thoroughly investigate all reports of harassment as discreetly and confidentially as practicable. The investigation would generally include a private interview with the person making a report of harassment. It would also generally be necessary to discuss allegations of harassment with the accused individual and others who may have information relevant to the investigation. Single Barrel Consulting, LLC' goal is to conduct a thorough investigation, to determine whether harassment occurred, and to determine what action to take if it is determined that improper behavior occurred.

If Single Barrel Consulting, LLC determines that a violation of this policy has occurred, it will take appropriate disciplinary action against the offending party, which can include counseling, warnings, suspensions, and termination. Employees who report violations of this policy and employees who cooperate with investigations into alleged violations of this policy will not be subject to retaliation. Upon completion of the investigation, Single Barrel Consulting, LLC will inform the employee who made the complaint of the results of the investigation.

Compliance with this policy is a condition of each employee's employment. Employees are encouraged to raise any questions or concerns about this policy or about possible discriminatory harassment with the management. In the case where the allegation of harassment is against the management, please notify the staff member designated as grievance officer.

VIII. FRATERNIZATION POLICY

Dating guests of the club is forbidden. All employees acknowledge that it is absolutely against the policy of the Company for any employee or Lessee of the club to date or socialize in any manner outside the premises of the Company with any customer of <u>Single Barrel Consulting, LLC</u>.

IX. SOLICITATION

Any spoken or written offer of sexual service, by you or a guest, in or outside of the club constitutes solicitation and is strictly against the law. Employees must never ask a guest to buy him/her a drink or food. Employees may not contract for private parties of any kind. Any guest found soliciting our employees will be asked to leave. Any employee found soliciting a guest shall be terminated. Employees are not allowed to leave with any guest for any reason. Dating any guest is STRICTLY AGAINST COMPANY POLICY.

X. HOURS OF WORK, ATTENDANCE, AND PUNCTUALITY

HOURS OF WORK. <u>Single Barrel Consulting, LLC</u> may be open to the public at any time from 11 am until 6 am, 365 days each year. Employees may request the opportunity to vary their work schedules (within employer-defined limits) to better accommodate personal responsibilities. Subject to <u>Single Barrel Consulting, LLC</u> work assignments management's approval, the employee's supervisor shall determine the hours of employment that best suits the needs of the work to be done by the individual employee.

ATTENDANCE AND PUNCTUALITY. Attendance is a key factor in your job performance. Punctuality and regular attendance are expected of all employees. Excessive absences (whether excused or unexcused), tardiness or leaving early is unacceptable. If you are absent for any reason or plan to arrive late or leave early, you must notify your supervisor and the office manager as far in advance as possible and no later than one hour before the start of your scheduled workday. In the event of an emergency, you must notify your supervisor as soon as possible.

For all absences extending longer than one day, you must telephone your immediate supervisor prior to the start of each scheduled workday. When reporting an absence, you should indicate the nature of the problem causing your absence and your expected return-to-work date. A physician's statement may be required as proof of the need for any illness-related absence regardless of the length of the absence. Except as provided in other policies, an employee who is absent from work for three consecutive days without notification to his or her supervisor or the Executive Director will be considered to have voluntarily terminated his or her employment. The employee's final paycheck will be mailed to the last mailing address on file with <u>Single Barrel Consulting, LLC</u>.

Excessive absences, tardiness or leaving early will be grounds for discipline up to and including termination. Depending on the circumstances, including the employee's length of employment, <u>Single Barrel Consulting, LLC</u> may counsel employees prior to termination for excessive absences, tardiness or leaving early.

OVERTIME. Overtime pay, which is applicable only to Non-Exempt Employees, is for any time worked in excess of 40 hours in a workweek or 12 hours in one day. Only the Executive Director or his or her designee, upon the request of an employee's supervisor, may authorize overtime. Overtime rate is one and one-half time (1½) the employee's straight time rate. Payment of overtime will be provided in the pay period following the period in which it is earned.

TIME CLOCK PROCEDURES. All employees (exempt and nonexempt) are required to use the time clock system to record his/her hours worked. Bartenders, Waitresses, Cashiers, Bar Backs, and Door Hosts are required to clock in and out on the Aloha System for payroll and attendance purposes. The time clock records will be used to track attendance for exempt employees.

WINDOW FOR CLOCKING IN AND OUT. Opening or relieving employees are to clock in no more than 15 minutes prior to their scheduled shift to receive banks, instructions, transfer tabs, and set up work area.

Last call times may vary. The manager will record the time last call is given. The doors are to be closed 30 minutes after last call is given. Door host should clock out once the doors are closed. Waitresses and Bartenders must clock out within 30 minutes of door closure. Bar Backs and Cashiers must clock out within 60 minutes of door closure.

If an employee misses the window for clocking into the timekeeping system, the employee should notify the supervisor as soon as possible. The supervisor will manually enter the employee's work hours via the manager time clock portal. Employees who repeatedly miss time clock entries will be subject to disciplinary action.

TIME CLOCK STATIONS. Employees are required to clock in and out on the Aloha Terminal located in their departments using their Aloha card or password. If there is a problem with the time clock, employees should notify their supervisor, and the supervisor will direct the employees to the next appropriate time clock station.

PROHIBITED ACTIONS. Accurately recording time worked is the responsibility of every employee. Employees may not use another employee's card to clock in or clock out for another employee. Tampering, altering, or falsifying time records, or recording time on another employee's time record may result in disciplinary action, including separation from employment with <u>Single Barrel Consulting, LLC</u>. Employees who have lost a card must report the lost card to the payroll department. The employee will be issued a new card with the same employee and department numbers.

Employees are permitted to work overtime only with prior authorization from their supervisors. Overtime includes clocking in early or late. Employees who work overtime without prior authorization will be subject to disciplinary procedures.

ENFORCEMENT. Supervisors are free to use discretion in disciplinary actions when employees have various, albeit repeated, offenses to the timekeeping policy or procedure. Situations include when employees may have clocked in, but are repeatedly absent from their workstations during work hours or have missed time clock entries in addition to working unscheduled overtime. Please refer to the Employee Disciplinary Action policy for direction on the appropriate disciplinary actions.

XI. EMPLOYMENT POLICIES AND PRACTICES
DEFINITION OF TERMS

- **Employer.** Single Barrel Consulting, LLC is the employer of all full-time, part-time and temporary employees. An employee is hired, provided compensation and applicable benefits, and has his or her work directed and evaluated by Single Barrel Consulting, LLC.
- **Full-Time Employee.** A Full-Time Employee regularly works at least 32 hours per week.
- **Part-Time Employee.** A Part Time Employee regularly works less than 32 hours per week.
- **Exempt Employee.** An Exempt Employee is an employee who is paid on a salary basis and meets the qualifications for exemption from the overtime requirements of the Fair Labor Standards Act ("FLSA").
- **Non-Exempt Employee.** A Non-Exempt Employee is an employee who is paid an hourly rate and does not meet the qualifications for exemption from the overtime requirements of the Fair Labor Standards Act ("FLSA"). For Non-Exempt Employees, an accurate record of hours worked must be maintained. Single Barrel Consulting, LLC will compensate non-exempt employees in accordance with applicable federal and state law and regulations.
- **Temporary Employee.** An individual employed, either on a full-time or part-time basis, for a specific period of time less than six months. Temporary employees are entitled only to those benefits required by statute or as otherwise stated in *The Employee Handbook.*

All employees are classified as Exempt or Non-Exempt in accordance with federal and state law and regulations. Each employee is notified at the time of hire of his or her specific compensation category and exempt or non-exempt status.

XII. POSITION DESCRIPTION AND SALARY ADMINISTRATION
Each position shall have a written job description. In general, the description will include the: purpose of the position, areas of responsibilities, immediate supervisor(s), qualifications required, salary range, and working conditions affecting the job, e.g., working hours, use of car, etc. The supervisor(s) or the Executive Director shall have discretion to modify the job description to meet the needs of Single Barrel Consulting, LLC.

The pay period is for two weeks and runs Monday through Sunday. Paychecks are distributed bimonthly, after 3:00 pm, on the Friday following the end of the pay period. Timesheets and Timecards are due before 10:00 am on the Monday following the end of the pay period. All salary deductions are itemized and presented to employees with his/her paycheck. Approved salary deductions may include federal and state income taxes; social security, Medicare, and state disability insurance; voluntary medical and group hospitalization insurance premiums (if in force and if paid by employee) and garnishments.

IMPORTANT TAX INFORMATION
It is imperative for the receipt of your correct W-2 that we have your correct name, address, and Social Security Number. The name on your W-4 must match exactly with the name on your Social Security card. If your name has changes due to marriage or divorce, you must apply for a new Social Security Card. Until we receive a photocopy of your new Social Security card, your paychecks will be issued under the name on your current card.

Changes and corrections can be made by mail or in person with the HR personnel in the office at 490 S. Colorado Blvd. Glendale, CO 80246

Generally, the more allowances you claim, the less tax will be withheld from your paycheck. The fewer allowances claimed, the larger withholding amount, which may result in a refund. If you wish to change your allowances, fill out a new W-4 and turn into the HR department.

TIP REPORTING
The reporting of tips is my responsibility and that I have been given the opportunity to report any tips received on a time card or electronic time clock. Per Colorado state law, employers may require employees to share or allocate tips and gratuities on a pre-established basis with other employees.

XIII. WORK REVIEW
The work of each employee is reviewed on an ongoing basis by the supervisors. The performance review may be informal but allows opportunity for the supervisor and employee to exchange ideas that will strengthen working relationships and anticipate Single Barrel Consulting, LLC' needs in the future. The purpose of the review is to encourage the exchange of ideas to create positive change within Single Barrel Consulting, LLC. To that end, it is incumbent upon both parties to have an open, and honest discussion concerning the employee's performance. It is further incumbent upon the supervisor to clearly communicate the needs of Single Barrel Consulting, LLC and what is expected of the employee.

Both supervisor and employee should attempt to arrive at an understanding regarding the objectives. This having been done, both parties should sign the performance review form, which will be kept as part of the employee's personnel record and used as a guide to monitor employee progress relative to the agreed upon objectives.

The Executive Director reviews the work of all supervisors. Work reviews for other staff are the responsibility of the appropriate supervisor, subject to confirmation by the Executive Director.

XIV. ECONOMIC BENEFITS AND INSURANCE

Single Barrel Consulting, LLC shall provide a competitive package of benefits to all eligible full-time employees. The following outline of available benefits is provided with the understanding that benefit plans may change from time to time. Single Barrel Consulting, LLC reserves the right to modify or terminate any employee benefits, at any time.

Plan brochures or contracts are to be considered the final word on the terms and conditions of the employee benefits provided by Single Barrel Consulting, LLC. The continuation of any benefits after termination of employment will be solely at the employee's expense, and only if permitted by policies and statutes. The Office Manager will determine levels of deductibility and co-payments for all insurance related benefits.

HEALTH INSURANCE. Single Barrel Consulting, LLC currently provides individual health insurance benefits for eligible full-time employees except those who choose to be insured through their spouse, retired military, or other plans, beginning after the third full month of employment.

Eligible employees may elect to participate in available health plan(s) offered by Single Barrel Consulting, LLC. Single Barrel Consulting, LLC presently pays 100% of the individual insurance premium for the Kaiser Bronze Plan. Single Barrel Consulting, LLC will require employees to pay a portion of insurance premium for other plans selected. Information about Single Barrel Consulting, LLC' health plan(s) will be provided to the employee at the time of eligibility.

SOCIAL SECURITY/MEDICAID/MEDICARE. Single Barrel Consulting, LLC participates in the provisions of the Social Security, Medicare and Medicaid programs. Employees' contributions are deducted from each paycheck and Single Barrel Consulting, LLC contributes at the applicable wage base as established by federal law. In the case of a zero $ check, the employee will be required to pay Single Barrel Consulting, LLC directly for his/her cost of the insurance premium.

WORKERS COMPENSATION & UNEMPLOYMENT INSURANCE. Employees are covered for benefits under the Worker's Compensation Law. Absences for which worker compensation benefits are provided are not charged against the eligible employee's sick leave. To assure proper protection for employees and Single Barrel Consulting, LLC, any accident that occurs on the job must be reported, even if there are no injuries apparent at the time. Forms for this purpose are available from the manager.

WORKERS COMPENSATION CLAIMS

All employees must obtain treatment of work-related injuries and illnesses from:

Medical Facility   Phone Number
Address, City, ST 00000
or
Medical Facility   Phone Number
Address, City, ST 00000

- In the event of a life-or-limb threatening emergency, the insured employee will be sent to the nearest emergency medical facility. The medical provider designated below must provide follow-up care.
- In the event of a non-emergency, after-hours injury, the provider should be called for access information and treatment instructions.
- The manager on duty must be notified and a first report of injury must be turned into the payroll office within 24 hours of injury. Contact the HR Department.
- The first Report of Injury is to be faxed to: xxx-xxx-xxxx. If an unauthorized medical provider treats an employee, the employee will be responsible for the payment of said treatment.

Single Barrel Consulting, LLC also participates in the [STATE] unemployment program.

XV. LEAVE BENEFITS AND OTHER WORK POLICIES
HOLIDAYS
Full-Time Employees are eligible for 2 of 8 unpaid holidays per year as follows:

New Year's Eve	Employee's Birthday	Memorial Day
Independence Day	Labor Day	Thanksgiving Day
Christmas Eve	Christmas Day	

Employees wishing to take religious holidays may substitute a religious holiday for one of those listed above, with advance approval from their supervisor or the Executive Director. Temporary and Part-time employees are ineligible for holiday leave benefits.

VACATIONS. All employees are eligible to take two weeks of unpaid vacation after one year of employment. Use of Vacation is subject to approval by the supervisor or Executive Director. Employees are granted three weeks unpaid vacation after 5 years of uninterrupted employment.

No vacation benefits are paid upon separation from employment with Single Barrel Consulting, LLC for any reason.

SICK LEAVE. Use of unpaid sick leave is subject to approval by the supervisor or the Executive Director and must be requested in daily increments. If an employee's illness or injury requires a consecutive absence of five (5) days or more, physician documentation will be required. Single Barrel Consulting, LLC also may recommend that the employee apply for state disability insurance (SDI).

No leave benefits are paid upon separation from employment with Single Barrel Consulting, LLC for any reason.

MILITARY LEAVE. Employees who are inducted into or enlist in the Armed Forces of the United States or are called to duty as a member of a reserve unit may take an unpaid leave in accordance with applicable law. The employee must provide notice of his or her need for a military leave and Single Barrel Consulting, LLC will request a copy of the employee's orders, which will be kept on record by Single Barrel Consulting, LLC.

The time an employee spends on military leave will be counted as continuous service for the purpose of determining eligibility and accrual for various benefit plans and policies.

For military leaves extending 30 days or less, <u>Single Barrel Consulting, LLC</u> will continue to pay the portion of the premium on health insurance, if any, that it was paying before military leave began. In order to continue such health insurance, the employee must continue to pay his or her portion of premiums during this period. For military leaves extending beyond 30 days, the employee will have the option to continue his or her insurance coverage at the employee's cost.

Upon return from military leave, employees will be reinstated as required by law and benefits will be reinstated with no waiting periods.

CIVIC RESPONSIBILITY. <u>Single Barrel Consulting, LLC</u> believes in the civic responsibility of its employees and encourages this by allowing employees time off to serve jury duty when required and to serve as nonpartisan Election Day poll workers when appropriate and approved.

- *Jury Duty.* For time served on jury duty, <u>Single Barrel Consulting, LLC</u> will pay employees the difference between his or her salary and any amount paid by the government, unless prohibited by law, up to a maximum of five days. If an employee is required to serve more than five days of jury duty, <u>Single Barrel Consulting, LLC</u> will provide the employee with unpaid leave. Employees must provide <u>Single Barrel Consulting, LLC</u> a copy of proof of service received by court in which they serve.
- *Election Day Poll Workers.* <u>Single Barrel Consulting, LLC</u> will allow leave but will not pay employees his or her salary for serving as an Election Day worker at the polls on official election days (not to exceed two elections in one given calendar year). <u>Single Barrel Consulting, LLC</u> requires that employees provide proof of service for their time at the polls. Employees interested in using this benefit, must have written approval from the management staff 30 days before the election. The Management staff will assure that the employee's absence will not seriously interfere with the organization's operations.

PARENTAL LEAVE. The Parental Leave Act entitles employees to certain unpaid parental leave. For purposes of this section only, the following definitions apply:

- "parent" means the natural mother or father of a child; a person who has legal custody of a child or who acts as a guardian of a child regardless of whether he or she has been appointed legally as such; an aunt, uncle or grandparent of a child; or a spouse to the above individuals;
- "school-related event" means an activity sponsored by either a school or an associated organization such as a parent-teacher association which involves the parent's child as a participant or subject, but not as a spectator, including a student performance, such as a concert, play or rehearsal, the sporting game of a school team or practice, a meeting with a teacher or counselor, or any similar type of activity.

A parent is entitled to a total of 24 hours of unpaid leave during any 12-month period to attend or participate in school-related events for his or her child. Single Barrel Consulting, LLC reserves the right, however, to deny such leave if such a leave would disrupt Single Barrel Consulting, LLC's operations.

If the need for parental leave is foreseeable, the employee must provide a written notice and request for parental leave at least 10 days prior to the event. If the employee's need for parental leave is not foreseeable 10 days prior to the event, the employee must provide a written notice and request for parental leave as soon as he or she learns of the need for such leave.

BEREAVMENT LEAVE. Employees shall be entitled to unpaid bereavement leave with pay of five (5) days in the event of a death in the employee's immediate family (spouse/life partner, child or parent) and three (3) days for grandparent, sister or brother, father-in-law, mother-in-law, or grandchildren. If an employee wishes to take time off due to the death of an immediate family member, the employee should notify the management Staff immediately. Approval of bereavement leave will occur in the absence of unusual operating requirements.

EXTENDED PERSONAL LEAVE. Employees who have been employed by Single Barrel Consulting, LLC for at least five years may apply for unpaid personal leaves of absence for up to eight weeks. Personal leaves are unpaid and are discretionary with the management of Single Barrel Consulting, LLC. When considering a request for a personal leave, Single Barrel Consulting, LLC will consider factors such as the employee's position, the employee's length of service, the employee's performance record including attendance, the purpose of the leave, the needs of the department in which the employee works, the effect of the leave on other employees, and the general business needs of Single Barrel Consulting, LLC.

Personal leaves generally are unpaid. However, Medical benefits will continue on the same basis as if the employee were actively working.

Single Barrel Consulting, LLC cannot guarantee reinstatement upon return from a personal leave. Single Barrel Consulting, LLC will, however, make a reasonable effort to place the employee in an available position for which he or she is qualified. If such a position is not available, then the employee's employment will terminate. Even in that event, the employee may later apply for reemployment.

Employees who fail to report to work after an approved leave of absence are deemed to have voluntarily resigned. When an approved leave has been exhausted, the employee may request additional leave. The Executive Director or management staff must approve all unpaid leave.

SEVERE WEATHER CONDITIONS. Single Barrel Consulting, LLC never closes due to severe weather; however, unpaid personal leave may be taken without prior scheduling and approval if the employee is unable to reach the office due to severe weather conditions. The employee is required to call the manager on duty and notify the club that the employee cannot make his/her shift for that day.

MEETINGS AND CONFERENCES. Staff may be given limited time off by the Executive Director with pay to participate in educational opportunities related to the staff member's current or anticipated work with <u>Single Barrel Consulting, LLC</u>. An employee serving as an official representative of <u>Single Barrel Consulting, LLC</u> at an approved conference or meeting is considered on official business and not on leave.

XVI. REIMBURSEMENT OF EXPENSES

Reimbursement is authorized for reasonable and necessary expenses incurred in carrying out job responsibilities. Mileage or transportation, parking fees, business telephone calls, and meal costs when required to attend a luncheon or banquet, are all illustrative of reasonable and necessary expenses.

Employees serving in an official capacity for <u>Single Barrel Consulting, LLC</u> at conferences and meetings are reimbursed for actual and necessary expenses incurred, such as travel expenses, meal costs, lodging, tips and registration fees. When attending meetings that have been approved by the Executive Director, employees are reimbursed for travel expenses, course fees, and costs of meals, and lodging at the current rates. Employees may also request a travel advance to cover anticipated expenses approved travel. Employees also may be granted leave to attend a conference or professional meeting related to their professional development, and/or <u>Single Barrel Consulting, LLC</u>' current and anticipated work. Expenses for these purposes may be paid by <u>Single Barrel Consulting, LLC</u>, if funds are available, and the employee obtains prior written approval of such expenses. Employees are responsible for transportation costs between the workplace and home during normal work hours.

Forms are provided to request reimbursement for actual expenses and advance payment for travel. Receipts must be provided for all expenditures made to claim reimbursement.

XVII. SEPARATION

Either <u>Single Barrel Consulting, LLC</u> or the employee may initiate separation. <u>Single Barrel Consulting, LLC</u> encourages employees to provide at least two weeks (10 days) written notice prior to intended separation for the purpose of training your replacement. After receiving such notice, an exit interview will be scheduled by the Executive Director or his or her designee. The Executive Director has authority to employ or separate all other employees. Circumstances under which separation may occur include:

RESIGNATION. Employees are encouraged to give at least 10 days of written notice. The intention to resign should be made known as far in advance as possible.

TERMINATION OR LAY-OFF. Under certain circumstances, the termination or lay-off of an employee may be necessary.

The Executive Director or her designee has the authority to discharge an employee from the employ of <u>Single Barrel Consulting, LLC</u>. As stated above, all employment at <u>Single Barrel Consulting, LLC</u> is "at-will." That means that employees may be terminated from employment with <u>Single Barrel Consulting, LLC</u> with or **without**

cause, and employees are free to leave the employment of <u>Single Barrel Consulting, LLC</u> with or **without cause**. Reasons for discharge may include, but are not limited to:

- Falsifying or withholding information on your employment application that did or would have affected <u>Single Barrel Consulting, LLC</u>' decision to hire you (this conduct will result in your immediate termination);
- Falsifying or withholding information in other personnel records including personnel questionnaires, performance evaluations or any other records;
- Performance at work below a level acceptable to <u>Single Barrel Consulting, LLC</u> or the failure to perform assigned duties;
- Failure to complete required time records or falsification of such time records;
- Insubordination;
- Refusing to work reasonable overtime;
- Negligence in the performance of duties likely to cause or causing personal injury or property damage;
- Fighting, arguing or attempting to injure another;
- Destroying or willfully damaging the personal property of another, including <u>Single Barrel Consulting, LLC</u>' property;
- Breach of confidentiality;
- Using or appearing to use for personal gain any information obtained on the job, which is not readily available to the general public or disclosing such information that damages the interests of <u>Single Barrel Consulting, LLC</u> or its customers or vendors;
- Placing oneself in a position in which personal interests and those of <u>Single Barrel Consulting, LLC</u> are or appear to be in conflict or might interfere with the ability of the employee to perform the job as well as possible;
- Using Company property or services for personal gain or taking, removing or disposing of Company material, supplies or equipment without proper authority;
- Gambling in any form on Company property;
- Dishonesty;
- Theft;
- The possession, use, sale or being under the influence of drugs or other controlled substances or alcoholic beverages during working hours or on Company premises at any time in violation of Company policies;
- Unapproved carrying or possessing firearms or weapons on Company property;
- Excessive tardiness or absenteeism whether excused or unexcused;
- Unauthorized absence from work without proper notice; and
- Engaging in discriminatory or abusive behavior, including sexual harassment.

At the sole discretion of the Executive Director or her designee, the employee may be asked to leave immediately or be given a period of notice.

XVIII. RETURN OF PROPERTY

Employees are responsible for Company equipment, property and work products that may be issued to them and/or are in their possession or control, including but not limited to:

- Mobile phone,
- Credit cards,
- Identification badges,
- Office/building keys,
- Office/building security passes,
- Computers, computerized diskettes, electronic/voice mail codes, and
- Intellectual property (e.g., written materials, work products).

In the event of separation from employment, or immediately upon request by the Executive Director or his or her designee, Employees must return all Company property that is in their possession or control. Where permitted by applicable law(s), Single Barrel Consulting, LLC may withhold from the employee's final paycheck the cost of any property, including intellectual property, which is not returned when required. Single Barrel Consulting, LLC also may take any action deemed appropriate to recover or protect its property.

XIX. PERSONNEL RECORDS

Employees may request a review of a personnel action or an unsatisfactory performance review. Employees are expected first to discuss their concern with their immediate supervisor. If further discussion is desired, the employee may then discuss the situation with the Human Resources Department followed by the Executive Director. The decision of the Executive Director is final.

Personnel records are the property of Single Barrel Consulting, LLC, and access to the information they contain is restricted and confidential. A personnel file shall be kept for each employee and should include the employee's job application, copy of the letter of employment and position description, performance reviews, disciplinary records, records of salary increases and any other relevant personnel information. It is the responsibility of each employee to promptly notify his/ or her supervisor in writing of any changes in personnel data, including personal mailing addresses, telephone numbers, names of dependents, and individuals to be contacted in the event of an emergency.

XX. OUTSIDE EMPLOYMENT

Individuals employed by Single Barrel Consulting, LLC may hold outside jobs as long as they meet the performance standards of their job with Single Barrel Consulting, LLC. Employees should consider the impact that outside employment may have on their ability to perform their duties at Single Barrel Consulting, LLC. All employees will be evaluated by the same performance standards and will be subject to Single Barrel Consulting, LLC scheduling demands, **regardless** of any outside work requirements. If Single Barrel Consulting, LLC' supervisor determines that an employee's outside work interferes with their job performance or their ability to meet the requirements of Single Barrel Consulting, LLC, as they are modified from time to time, the employee may be asked to terminate the outside employment if he or she wishes to remain employed with Single Barrel Consulting, LLC.

Outside employment that constitutes a conflict of interest is prohibited. Employees may not receive any income or material gain from individuals or organizations for materials produced or services rendered while performing their jobs with Single Barrel Consulting, LLC.

XXI. NON-DISCLOSURE OF CONFIDENTIAL INFORMATION

Any information that an employee learns about Single Barrel Consulting, LLC, or its members or donors, as a result of working for Single Barrel Consulting, LLC that is not otherwise publicly available constitutes confidential information. Employees may not disclose confidential information to anyone who is not employed by Single Barrel Consulting, LLC or to other persons employed by Single Barrel Consulting, LLC who do not need to know such information to assist in rendering services.

The protection of privileged and confidential information, including trade secrets, is vital to the interests and the success of Single Barrel Consulting, LLC. The disclosure, distribution, electronic transmission or copying of Single Barrel Consulting, LLC' confidential information is prohibited. Such information includes, but is not limited to, the following examples: compensation data, programs, and/or financial information, including information related to vendors, guests, or donors, and/or pending projects and proposals that are the sole property of Single Barrel Consulting, LLC.

Employees may be required to sign an additional non-disclosure agreement as a condition of employment. Any employee who discloses confidential Company information will be subject to disciplinary action (including separation), even if he or she does not actually benefit from the disclosure of such information.

Discussions involving sensitive information should always be held in confidential settings to safeguard the confidentiality of the information. Conversations regarding confidential information generally should not be conducted on cellular phones, or in elevators, restrooms, restaurants, or other places where conversations might be overheard.

XXII. COMPUTER AND INFORMATION SECURITY

This section sets forth some important rules relating to the use of Company computers and communications systems. These systems include individual PCs provided to employees, centralized computer equipment, all associated software, and Company telephones, voice mail and electronic mail systems.

Single Barrel Consulting, LLC has provided these systems to support its mission. Although limited personal use of Company systems is allowed, subject to the restrictions outlined below, no use of these systems should ever conflict with the primary purpose for which they have been provided, Single Barrel Consulting, LLC' ethical responsibilities or with applicable laws and regulations. Each user is personally responsible to ensure that these guidelines are followed.

All data in Single Barrel Consulting, LLC' computer and communication systems (including documents, other electronic files, e-mail and recorded voice mail messages) are the property of Single Barrel Consulting, LLC. Single Barrel Consulting, LLC may inspect and monitor such data at any time. No individual should have any expectation of privacy for messages or other data recorded in <u>Single Barrel Consulting, LLC</u>' systems. This includes documents or messages marked "private," which may be inaccessible to most users but remain available to <u>Single Barrel Consulting, LLC</u>. Likewise, the deletion of a document or message may not prevent access to the item or eliminate the item from the system.

<u>Single Barrel Consulting, LLC</u>' systems must not be used to create or transmit material that is derogatory, defamatory, obscene or offensive, such as slurs, epithets or anything that might be construed as harassment or disparagement based on race, color, national origin, sex, sexual orientation, age, physical or mental disability, medical condition, marital status, or religious or political beliefs. Similarly, <u>Single Barrel Consulting, LLC</u>' systems must not be used to solicit or proselytize others for commercial purposes, causes, outside organizations, chain messages or other non-job-related purposes.

Security procedures in the form of unique user sign-on identification and passwords have been provided to control access to <u>Single Barrel Consulting, LLC</u>' host computer system, networks and voice mail system. In addition, security facilities have been provided to restrict access to certain documents and files for the purpose of safeguarding information.

The following activities present security risks and should be avoided:
- Attempts should not be made to bypass, or render ineffective, security facilities provided by <u>Single Barrel Consulting, LLC</u>.
- Confidential Passwords should not be shared between users. If written down, password should be kept in locked drawers or other places not easily accessible.
- Individual users should never make changes or modifications to the hardware configuration of computer equipment. Requests for such changes should be directed to computer support.
- Document libraries of other users should not be browsed unless there is a legitimate business reason.
- Additions to or modifications of the standard software configuration provided on <u>Single Barrel Consulting, LLC</u>' PCs should never be attempted by individual users (e.g., autoexec.bat and config.sys files). Requests for such changes should be directed to computer support.
- Programs should never be downloaded from bulletin board systems or copied from other computers outside <u>Single Barrel Consulting, LLC</u> onto company computers. Downloading or copying such programs also risks the introduction of a computer virus. If there is a need for such programs, a request for assistance should be directed to computer support or management. Downloading or copying documents from outside <u>Single Barrel Consulting, LLC</u> may be performed not to present a security risk.
- Users should not attempt to boot PCs from floppy diskettes. This practice also risks the introduction of a computer virus.
- <u>Single Barrel Consulting, LLC</u>' computer facilities should not be used to attempt unauthorized access to or use of other organizations' computer systems and data.

- Computer games should not be loaded on <u>Single Barrel Consulting, LLC</u>' PCs.
- Unlicensed software should not be loaded or executed on <u>Single Barrel Consulting, LLC</u>' PCs.
- Company software (whether developed internally or licensed) should not be copied onto floppy diskettes or other media other than for the purpose of backing up your hard drive. Software documentation for programs developed and/or licensed by <u>Single Barrel Consulting, LLC</u> should not be removed from <u>Single Barrel Consulting, LLC</u>' offices.
- Individual users should not change the location or installation of computer equipment in offices and work areas. Requests for such changes should be directed to computer support or management.

There are several practices that individual users should adopt that will foster a higher level of security. Among them are the following:
- Turn off your personal computer when you are leaving your work area or office for an extended period.
- Exercise judgment in assigning an appropriate level of security to documents stored on <u>Single Barrel Consulting, LLC</u>' networks, based on a realistic appraisal of the need for confidentiality or privacy.
- Remove previously written information from floppy diskettes before copying documents on such diskettes for delivery outside <u>Single Barrel Consulting, LLC</u>.
- Back up any information stored locally on your personal computer (other than network-based software and documents) on a frequent and regular basis.
- Should you have any questions about any of the above policy guidelines, please contact the Human Resources Department or the Executive Director.

XXIII. INTERNET ACCEPTABLE USE POLICY

Currently, desktop access to the Internet is provided to employees when there is a necessity and the access has been specifically approved. <u>Single Barrel Consulting, LLC</u> has provided access to the Internet for authorized users to support its mission. No use of the Internet should conflict with the primary purpose of <u>Single Barrel Consulting, LLC</u>, its ethical responsibilities or with applicable laws and regulations. Each user is personally responsible to ensure that these guidelines are followed. Serious repercussions, including termination, may result if the guidelines are not followed.

<u>Single Barrel Consulting, LLC</u> may monitor usage of the Internet by employees, including reviewing a list of sites accessed by an individual. No individual should have any expectation of privacy in terms of his or her usage of the Internet. In addition, <u>Single Barrel Consulting, LLC</u> may restrict access to certain sites that it deems are not necessary for business purposes.

<u>Single Barrel Consulting, LLC</u>' connection to the Internet may not be used for any of the following activities:
- The Internet must not be used to access, create, transmit, print or download material that is derogatory, defamatory, obscene, or offensive, such as slurs, epithets, or anything that may be construed as harassment or disparagement based on race, color, national origin, sex, sexual orientation, age, disability,

medical condition, marital status, or religious or political beliefs with exception for promotional activity designated by the promotions department.

- The Internet must not be used to access, send, receive, or solicit sexually oriented messages or images with exception for promotional activity designated by the promotions department.
- Downloading or disseminating of copyrighted material that is available on the Internet is an infringement of copyright law. Permission to copy the material must be obtained from the publisher. For assistance with copyrighted material, contact computer support or the manager.
- Without prior approval of the Office manager, software should not be downloaded from the Internet as the download could introduce a computer virus onto Single Barrel Consulting, LLC' computer equipment. In addition, copyright laws may cover the software so the downloading could be an infringement of copyright law.
- Employees should safeguard against using the Internet to transmit personal comments or statements through e-mail or to post information to news groups that may be mistaken as the position of Single Barrel Consulting, LLC.
- Employees should guard against the disclosure of confidential information using Internet e-mail or news groups.
- Employees should not download personal e-mail or Instant Messaging software to Single Barrel Consulting, LLC computers.
- The Internet should not be used to send or participate in chain letters, pyramid schemes or other illegal schemes.
- The Internet should not be used to solicit or proselytize others for commercial purposes, causes, outside organizations, chain messages or other non-job-related purposes.
- The Internet should not be used to endorse political candidates or campaigns
- The Internet provides access to many sites that charge a subscription or usage fee to access and use the information on the site. Requests for approval must be submitted to your supervisor.

XXIV. CIGAR BAR ACKNOWLEDGMENT

Single Barrel Consulting, LLC is a smoking environment. Employees further acknowledge that exposure to tobacco smoke may be harmful to his/her health. By voluntarily choosing to work in a smoking environment, All employees assume the risk of harm that may come from exposure to environmental smoke and hold harmless Single Barrel Consulting, LLC which has offered these individuals said employment. This acknowledgment in no way modifies any status as an at-will employee.

XXV. DRUG-FREE WORKPLACE POLICY

It is the policy of the Company to create a drug-free workplace. The illegal use of controlled substances is inconsistent with the behavior expected of employees and Lessees, subjects all employees, Lessees and clients to unacceptable safety risks and undermines the Company's ability to operate effectively and efficiently. In this connection, the unlawful manufacture, distribution, dispensation, possession, sale, or use of a controlled substance on Company property or while engaged in Company business off premises is strictly prohibited.

We do not allow the use of Cannabis, Marijuana, or THC products while you are working at Company property. It is strictly forbidden to bring in or store these products or any controlled substance on company property without a prescription.

To educate employees and Lessees on the dangers of drug abuse, the Company has conducted drug-free training sessions in the past. Periodically, employees may be required to attend training sessions at which the dangers of drug abuse, company policy regarding drugs and the availability of counseling may be discussed. These training sessions are open to Lessees but are not required.

Employees or Lessees who violate any aspect of this policy may be subject to disciplinary action up to and including, respectively, termination of their employment or lease. At its discretion, the management may require employees (but not Lessees) who violate this policy to successfully complete a drug abuse assistance or rehabilitation program as a condition of continued employment.

The Company reserves the right to require employees (but not Lessees) to undergo appropriate tests designed to detect the presents of alcohol, illegal drugs, or other controlled substances where it has reason to believe that an employee may be under the influences of any of these substances or as part of a random test of employees. Each employee is expected to cooperate and consent as a condition of continued employment. Refusal to consent to such testing may result in disciplinary action up to and including termination. We appreciate your help in keeping our club safe and drug free.

XXVI. <u>SINGLE BARREL CONSULTING, LLC</u> SAFETY POLICY

These general rules are designed to provide you with knowledge of the recognized and established safe practices and procedures that apply to many of the workstations you may encounter while employed with <u>Single Barrel Consulting, LLC</u>. It would be impossible to cover every situation. If you are in doubt about the safety of any condition, practice, or procedure consult your supervisor for guidance.

- **Accidents and Hazards:** Employees are responsible for notifying a supervisor immediately of any unsafe condition. Report all accidence or near misses to your supervisor before the end of your shift. Falsification of company records, including employment applications, time records, or safety documentation will not be tolerated.
- **Alcohol and Drugs:** Employees are to notify a supervisor of any prescription drugs that might affect the employees' judgment. The use of illegal drugs or alcohol while on shift will not be tolerated.
- **Seatbelts:** All employees who drive or travel on company time must use seat belts.
- **Horseplay:** Wrestling, running, pushing or other disorderly conduct is forbidden.
- **Drinking Water:** Always drink from regular water fountains or approved coolers.
- **Housekeeping:** All employees are required to keep their work areas clear of free of debris or other tripping or slipping hazards. Dispose of debris in the designated area.

- **Machinery:** You must have instruction from a supervisor before operating any unfamiliar machinery. Report broken or malfunctioning equipment to your supervisor. All electrical equipment will be disconnected from the power source if a malfunction is detected. Only trained, authorized employees are permitted to service or repair equipment.
- **Hazardous Materials:** You must have instruction from a supervisor before using any unfamiliar chemical. Follow proper use and handling procedures for all hazardous materials. Always wear protective gear.
- **Hygiene:** It is the employees' responsibility to maintain personal hygiene when working with hazardous materials. Eat and smoke only in designated areas. Always wash your hands before and after you eat or smoke.
- **Concentrate:** Most accidents can be avoided or reduced by concentrating on the job to be done. Be aware of your surroundings. Pay attention to all safety signs and labels. Safety is a full-time job.

If you have any questions regarding any of the policy guidelines listed above, please contact your supervisor or the Executive Director.

Revised 00/00/0000
Approved by the Executive Committee of <u>Single Barrel Consulting, LLC</u> Board of Directors

NEW HIRE PACKAGE

Your new hire packet will contain duplicates of several policies listed in your policy manual. In the new hire packet there will be spaces for the new employees to print and sign their name acknowledging they are aware of said policies. There is also a conclusion page stating they have read and fully understand the policy manual.

Contents

PERSONAL INFORMATION

HIRE DATE __________   DEPARTMENT __________   POSITION __________

NAME __________
LAST   FIRST   MI

ADDRESS __________
STREET   APT.

____
CITY   STATE   ZIP

PHONE __________   DATE OF BIRTH __________

EMAIL __________

GENDER   ETHNIC BACKGROUND (OTIONAL)
M ☐   ☐ BLACK OR AFRICAN AMERICAN   ☐ PACIFIC ISLANDER   ☐ CAUCASIAN
F ☐   ☐ AMERICAN INDIAN OR ALASKA NATIVE   ☐ LATINO OR HISPANIC   ☐ ASIAN

DRIVER'S LICENSE # __________
STATE   EXP

M.E.D. LICENSE # __________   SOCIAL SECURITY __________

ARE YOU A FORMER EMPLOYEE?   Y ☐   N ☐   IF SO, WHEN DID YOU LAST WORK? __________

WHY DID YOU LEAVE? __________

____

EMERGENCY CONTACT __________   PHONE __________

RELATIONSHIP __________

TO BE COMPLETED BY HIRING MANAGER

Direct Deposit ☐   Rate __________   Fulltime ☐   Partime ☐   Department __________

IMPORTANT TAX INFORMATION

It is imperative for the receipt of your correct W-2 that we have your correct name, address, and Social Security number. The name on your W-4 must match exactly with the name on your Social Security card. If your name has changed due to marriage or divorce, you must apply for a new Social Security card. Until we receive a photocopy of your new Social Security card, your paychecks will be issued under the name on your current card.

Changes and corrections can be made by mail or in-person with the HR personnel in the office at 490 S. Colorado Blvd. Glendale, CO 80246

Generally, the more allowances you claim, the less tax monies will be withheld from your paycheck. The fewer allowances claimed, the larger the withholding amount, which may result in a refund. If you wish to change your allowances, fill out a new W-4 and turn it into the HR department.

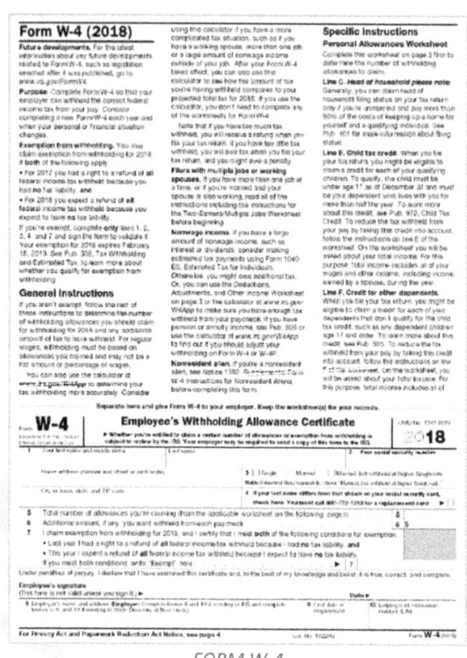

FORM W-4

TIP REPORTING

I, ____,
understand that the reporting of tips is my responsibility and that I have been given the opportunity to report any tips received on a time card or electronic time clock. According to Colorado state law, employers may require employees to share or allocate tips and gratuities on a pre-established basis with other employees.

________________________________   ________________________________
Print Name   Signature

FORM I-9

	Employment Eligibility Verification	**USCIS**
	Department of Homeland Security	**Form I-9**
	U.S. Citizenship and Immigration Services	OMB No. 1615-0047 Expires 10/31/2022

►START HERE: Read instructions carefully before completing this form. The instructions must be available, either in paper or electronically, during completion of this form. Employers are liable for errors in the completion of this form.

ANTI-DISCRIMINATION NOTICE: It is illegal to discriminate against work-authorized individuals. Employers **CANNOT** specify which document(s) an employee may present to establish employment authorization and identity. The refusal to hire or continue to employ an individual because the documentation presented has a future expiration date may also constitute illegal discrimination.

Section 1. Employee Information and Attestation *(Employees must complete and sign Section 1 of Form I-9 no later than the first day of employment, but not before accepting a job offer.)*

Last Name *(Family Name)*	First Name *(Given Name)*	Middle Initial	Other Last Names Used *(if any)*

Address *(Street Number and Name)*	Apt. Number	City or Town	State	ZIP Code

Date of Birth *(mm/dd/yyyy)*	U.S. Social Security Number	Employee's E-mail Address	Employee's Telephone Number

I am aware that federal law provides for imprisonment and/or fines for false statements or use of false documents in connection with the completion of this form.

I attest, under penalty of perjury, that I am (check one of the following boxes):

☐ 1. A citizen of the United States

☐ 2. A noncitizen national of the United States *(See instructions)*

☐ 3. A lawful permanent resident   (Alien Registration Number/USCIS Number): _______________

☐ 4. An alien authorized to work   until (expiration date, if applicable, mm/dd/yyyy): _______________
Some aliens may write "N/A" in the expiration date field. *(See instructions)*

Aliens authorized to work must provide only one of the following document numbers to complete Form I-9:
An Alien Registration Number/USCIS Number OR Form I-94 Admission Number OR Foreign Passport Number.

QR Code - Section 1
Do Not Write In This Space

1. Alien Registration Number/USCIS Number: _______________
OR
2. Form I-94 Admission Number: _______________
OR
3. Foreign Passport Number: _______________
Country of Issuance: _______________

Signature of Employee	Today's Date *(mm/dd/yyyy)*

Preparer and/or Translator Certification (check one):
☐ I did not use a preparer or translator   ☐ A preparer(s) and/or translator(s) assisted the employee in completing Section 1.
(Fields below must be completed and signed when preparers and/or translators assist an employee in completing Section 1.)

I attest, under penalty of perjury, that I have assisted in the completion of Section 1 of this form and that to the best of my knowledge the information is true and correct.

Signature of Preparer or Translator	Today's Date *(mm/dd/yyyy)*

Last Name *(Family Name)*	First Name *(Given Name)*

Address *(Street Number and Name)*	City or Town	State	ZIP Code

STOP *Employer Completes Next Page* **STOP**

Form I-9 10/21/2019

Page 1 of 3

Employment Eligibility Verification

Department of Homeland Security

U.S. Citizenship and Immigration Services

USCIS

Form I-9

OMB No. 1615-0047

Expires 10/31/2022

Section 2. Employer or Authorized Representative Review and Verification

(Employers or their authorized representative must complete and sign Section 2 within 3 business days of the employee's first day of employment. You must physically examine one document from List A OR a combination of one document from List B and one document from List C as listed on the "Lists of Acceptable Documents.")

Employee Info from Section 1	Last Name *(Family Name)*	First Name *(Given Name)*	M.I.	Citizenship/Immigration Status

List A Identity and Employment Authorization	OR	List B Identity	AND	List C Employment Authorization

List A	List B	List C
Document Title	Document Title	Document Title
Issuing Authority	Issuing Authority	Issuing Authority
Document Number	Document Number	Document Number
Expiration Date *(if any) (mm/dd/yyyy)*	Expiration Date *(if any) (mm/dd/yyyy)*	Expiration Date *(if any) (mm/dd/yyyy)*
Document Title		
Issuing Authority	Additional Information	QR Code - Sections 2 & 3 Do Not Write in This Space
Document Number		
Expiration Date *(if any) (mm/dd/yyyy)*		
Document Title		
Issuing Authority		
Document Number		
Expiration Date *(if any) (mm/dd/yyyy)*		

Certification: I attest, under penalty of perjury, that (1) I have examined the document(s) presented by the above-named employee, (2) the above-listed document(s) appear to be genuine and to relate to the employee named, and (3) to the best of my knowledge the employee is authorized to work in the United States.

The employee's first day of employment *(mm/dd/yyyy)*: ________________ *(See instructions for exemptions)*

Signature of Employer or Authorized Representative	Today's Date *(mm/dd/yyyy)*	Title of Employer or Authorized Representative
Last Name of Employer or Authorized Representative	First Name of Employer or Authorized Representative	Employer's Business or Organization Name

Employer's Business or Organization Address *(Street Number and Name)*	City or Town	State	ZIP Code

Section 3. Reverification and Rehires *(To be completed and signed by employer or authorized representative.)*

A. New Name *(if applicable)*			B. Date of Rehire *(if applicable)*
Last Name *(Family Name)*	First Name *(Given Name)*	Middle Initial	Date *(mm/dd/yyyy)*

C. If the employee's previous grant of employment authorization has expired, provide the information for the document or receipt that establishes continuing employment authorization in the space provided below.

Document Title	Document Number	Expiration Date *(if any) (mm/dd/yyyy)*

I attest, under penalty of perjury, that to the best of my knowledge, this employee is authorized to work in the United States, and if the employee presented document(s), the document(s) I have examined appear to be genuine and to relate to the individual.

Signature of Employer or Authorized Representative	Today's Date *(mm/dd/yyyy)*	Name of Employer or Authorized Representative

Form I-9 10/21/2019

Page 2 of 3

VOLUNTARY AT-WILL EMPLOYMENT

Unless an employee has a written employment agreement with <u>Single Barrel Consulting</u>, which provides differently, all employment at <u>Single Barrel Consulting</u> is "at-will."

That means that employees may be terminated from employment with <u>Single Barrel Consulting</u> with or without cause, and employees are free to leave the employment of <u>Single Barrel Consulting</u> with or without cause. Any representation by any <u>Single Barrel Consulting's</u> officer or employee contrary to this policy is not binding upon <u>Single Barrel Consulting</u> unless it is in writing and is signed by the Executive Director with the approval of the Board of Directors.

_______________________________   _______________________________

Print Name   Signature

EQUAL EMPLOYMENT OPPORTUNITY

Single Barrel Consulting, LLC shall follow the spirit and intent of all federal, state and local employment law and is committed to equal employment opportunity. To that end, the Board of Directors and Executive Director of Single Barrel Consulting will not discriminate against any employee or applicant in a manner that violates the law. Single Barrel Consulting is committed to providing equal opportunity for all employees and applicants without regard to race, color, religion, national origin, sex, age, marital status, sexual orientation, disability, political affiliation, personal appearance, family responsibilities, matriculation or any other characteristic protected under federal, state or local law. Each person is evaluated on the basis of personal skill and merit. Single Barrel Consulting's policy regarding equal employment opportunity applies to all aspects of employment, including recruitment, hiring, job assignments, promotions, working conditions, scheduling, benefits, wage and salary administration, disciplinary action, termination, and social, educational and recreational programs. The Executive Director shall act as the responsible agent in the full implementation of the Equal Employment Opportunity policy.

Single Barrel Consulting will not tolerate any form of unlawful discrimination. All employees are expected to cooperate fully in implementing this policy. In particular, any employee who believes that any other employee of Single Barrel Consulting may have violated the Equal Employment Opportunity Policy should report the possible violation to the Executive Director.

If Single Barrel Consulting determines that a violation of this policy has occurred, it will take appropriate disciplinary action against the offending party, which can include counseling, warnings, suspensions, and termination. Employees who report, in good faith, violations of this policy and employees who cooperate with investigations into alleged violations of this policy will not be subject to retaliation. Upon completion of the investigation, Single Barrel Consulting will inform the employee who made the complaint of the results of the investigation.

Single Barrel Consulting is also committed to complying fully with applicable disability discrimination laws, and ensuring that equal opportunity in employment exists at Single Barrel Consulting for qualified persons with disabilities. All employment practices and activities are conducted on a non-discriminatory basis. Reasonable accommodations will be available to all qualified disabled employees, upon request, so long as the potential accommodation does not create an undue hardship on Single Barrel Consulting. Employees who believe that they may require an accommodation should discuss these needs with the Executive Director.

SEXUAL HARASSMENT POLICY

It is the policy of <u>Single Barrel Consulting</u> that all employees and Lessees have the right to work in an environment free of discrimination, which encompasses freedom from sexual harassment. <u>Single Barrel Consulting</u> will not tolerate sexual harassment by anyone, male or female, even in the absence of a formal complaint. Such conduct may result in disciplinary action up to and including dismissal (for employees) or Lease termination (for Lessees).

Specifically, no supervisor or manager shall threaten or insinuate, either explicitly or implicitly, that an employee's or Lessees' submission to or rejection of sexual advances will in any way influence any decision regarding that individual's continuing relationship with <u>Single Barrel Consulting</u>.

Other sexually harassing conduct in the workplace, whether physical or verbal, committed by supervisory or non-supervisory personnel, or Lessees is also prohibited. This may include, but is not limited to: repeated offensive sexual flirtation; advances; propositions; leering, whistling, touching, pinching, or brushing of the body; continual or repeated verbal abuse of a sexual nature; graphic verbal commentaries about an individual; sexually degrading words used to describe an individual; jokes of a sexual nature and the display in the workplace of sexually suggestive objects or pictures.

Employees or Lessees who feel they have experienced or witnessed sexual harassment must immediately report such conduct to a manager. If the employee or Lessee is uncomfortable bringing the matter to his or her manager for any reason, the employee should seek the assistance of another manager or Deborah Matthews.

<u>Single Barrel Consulting</u> will promptly and thoroughly investigate all claims of sexual harassment to the fullest extent practicable. <u>Single Barrel Consulting</u> will keep complaints and the terms of the resolution confidential. Where investigation confirms the allegations, appropriate corrective action will be taken. <u>Single Barrel Consulting</u> forbids retaliation against anyone who reports harassment in good faith.

Having read and understood the foregoing, I knowingly agree to accept the <u>Single Barrel Consulting's</u> policy concerning discrimination and sexual harassment.

_______________________________ _______________________________
Print Name   Signature

SAFETY AND WORKER COMPENSATION POLICY

It is the policy of <u>Single Barrel Consulting</u> that the safety of its employees and the public is of chief importance. The prevention of accidents and injuries takes precedence over expedience. In the conduct of our business, every attempt will be made to prevent accidence from occurring. The company requires that its employees, as a condition of employment, comply with all applicable safety regulations as listed in the policy manual.

The designated safety coordinator for <u>Single Barrel Consulting</u> is the primary contact for safety-related matters. All employees will receive an orientation to the safety rules and policies of <u>Single Barrel Consulting</u> upon initial employment and through regular safety meeting throughout the year. Employees are encouraged to bring any unsafe practices or conditions to the attention of their immediate supervisor. The supervisor will relay these concerns to the safety coordinator, who will respond within 24 hours.

WHEN INJURED ON THE JOB

Employees are covered for benefits under the Worker's Compensation Law. Absences for which worker compensation benefits are provided are not charged against the eligible employee's sick leave if applicable. To assure proper protection for employees and <u>Single Barrel Consulting</u>, any accident that occurs on the job must be reported, even if there are no injuries apparent at the time. Forms for this purpose are available from the manager.

All employees must obtain treatment of work-related injuries and illnesses from a designated medical provider:

	-or-
Medical Facility	Medical Facility
Address	Address
City, ST Zip Code	City, ST Zip Code

In the event of a life-or-limb threatening emergency, the insured employee will be sent to the nearest emergency medical facility. The designated medical provider must provide follow-up care.

In the event of a non-emergency, after-hours injury, the provider should be called at (xxx) XXX-XXXX for access information and treatment instructions.

FIRST REPORT OF INJURY

The manager on duty must be notified and a first report of injury must be submitted to the payroll office within 24 hours of injury. Contact XXXX XXXXX at (xxx) XXX-XXXX for questions. The first Report of Injury is to be faxed to: (xxx) XXX-XXXX.

If an unauthorized medical provider treats an employee, the employee will be responsible for the payment of said treatment.

I have read and am fully aware of <u>Single Barrel Consulting, LLC's</u> policy regarding medical treatment for work-related injuries.

____

Print Name   Signature

COMPANY SAFETY POLICIES

These general rules are designed to provide you with knowledge of the recognized and established safe practices and procedures that apply to many of the work stations you may encounter while employed with <u>Single Barrel Consulting, LLC</u>. It would be impossible to cover every situation. If you are in doubt about the safety of any condition, practice, or procedure consult your supervisor for guidance.

Accidents and Hazards: Employees are responsible for notifying a supervisor immediately of any unsafe condition. Report all accidence or near misses to your supervisor before the end of your shift. Falsification of company records, including employment applications, time records, or safety documentation will not be tolerated.

Alcohol and Drugs: Employees are to notify a supervisor of any prescription drugs that might affect the employees' judgment. The use of illegal drugs or alcohol while on shift will not be tolerated.

Seatbelts: All employees who drive or travel on company time must use seat belts.

Horseplay: Wrestling, running, pushing or other disorderly conduct is forbidden.

Drinking Water: Always drink from regular water fountains or approved coolers.

Housekeeping: All employees are required to keep their work areas clear of free of trash or other tripping or slipping hazards. Dispose of debris in the designated area.

Machinery: You must have instruction from a supervisor before operating any unfamiliar machinery. Report broken or malfunctioning equipment to your supervisor. All electrical equipment will be disconnected from the power source if a malfunction is detected. Only trained, authorized employees or permitted to service or repair equipment.

Hazardous Materials: You must have instruction from a supervisor before using any unfamiliar chemical. Follow proper use and handling procedures for all hazardous materials. Always wear protective gear.

Hygiene: It is the employees' responsibility to maintain personal hygiene when working with hazardous materials. Eat and smoke only in designated areas. Always wash your hands before and after you eat or smoke.

Concentrate: Most accidents can be avoided or reduced by concentrating on the job to be done. Be aware of your surroundings. Pay attention to all safety signs and labels. Safety is a full-time job.

I ____ have read and understand the safety rules of <u>Single Barrel Consulting, LLC</u>. I agree to act in accordance with the safety rules at all times. I understand any violation of the safety rules is cause for disciplinary action up to and including termination of employment.

___________________________________   ___________________________________

Print Name   Signature

TIME-CLOCK PROCEDURES AND POLICIES

All employees (exempt and nonexempt) are required to use the time clock system to record hours worked. Bartenders, Waitresses, Cashiers, Bar Backs, and Door Hosts are required to clock in and out on the Aloha System for payroll and attendance purposes. The time clock records will be used to track attendance for exempt employees.

Opening or relieving employees and employees of <u>Single Barrel Consulting</u> are to clock in no more than 15 minutes prior to their scheduled shift to receive banks, instructions, transfer tabs, and set up work area.
Last call times may vary. The manager will record the time last call is given. The doors are to be closed 30 minutes after last call is given. Door host should clock out once the doors are closed. Waitresses and Bartenders must clock out within 30 minutes of door closure. Bar Backs and Cashiers must clock out within 60 minutes of door closure.

If an employee misses the window for clocking into the timekeeping system, the employee should notify the supervisor as soon as possible. The supervisor will manually enter the employee's work hours via the manager time clock portal. Employees who repeatedly miss time clock entries will be subject to disciplinary action.

TIME CLOCK STATIONS

Employees are required to clock in and out on the Aloha Terminal or BioTrack computer located in their departments using their Aloha card or password. If there is a problem with the time clock, employees should notify their supervisor, and the supervisor will direct the employees to the next appropriate time clock station.

PROHIBITED TIME CLOCK ACTIONS

Employees may not use another employee's card to clock in or clock out for another employee. Employees who have lost a card must report the lost card to the payroll department. The employee will be issued a new card with the same employee and department numbers.

OVERTIME

Employees are permitted to work overtime only with prior authorization from their supervisors. Overtime includes clocking in early or late. Employees who work overtime without prior authorization will be subject to disciplinary procedures.

ENFORCEMENT

Supervisors are free to use discretion in disciplinary actions when employees have various, albeit repeated, offenses to the timekeeping policy or procedure. Situations include when employees may have clocked in, but are repeatedly absent from their workstations during work hours or have missed time clock entries in addition to working unscheduled overtime. Please refer to the Employee Disciplinary Action policy for direction on the appropriate disciplinary actions.

____

Print Name

____

Signature

____

Department

DRUG-FREE WORKPLACE POLICY
It is the policy of <u>Single Barrel Consulting, LLC</u> to create a drug-free workplace. The illegal use of controlled substances is inconsistent with the behavior expected of employees and Lessees, subjects all employees, Lessees and clients to unacceptable safety risks and undermines <u>Single Barrel Consulting, LLC's</u> ability to operate effectively and efficiently. In this connection, the unlawful manufacture, distribution, dispensation, possession, sale, or use of a controlled substance on <u>Single Barrel Consulting, LLC</u> property or while engaged in <u>Single Barrel Consulting, LLC</u> business off premises is strictly prohibited.

We do not allow the use of Cannabis, Marijuana, or THC products while you are working on <u>Single Barrel Consulting, LLC</u> property. It is strictly forbidden to bring in or store these products or any controlled substance on company property without a prescription.

To educate employees and Lessees on the dangers of drug abuse, <u>Single Barrel Consulting</u> has conducted drug-free training sessions in the past. Periodically, employees may be required to attend training sessions at which the dangers of drug abuse, company policy regarding drugs and the availability of counseling may be discussed. These training sessions are open to Lessees, but are not required.

Employees or Lessees who violate any aspect of this policy may be subject to disciplinary action up to and including, respectively, termination of their employment or lease. At its discretion, the management may require employees (but not Lessees) who violate this policy to successfully complete a drug abuse assistance or rehabilitation program as a condition of continued employment.

<u>Single Barrel Consulting</u> reserves the right to require employees (but not Lessees) to undergo appropriate tests designed to detect the presents of alcohol, illegal drugs, or other controlled substances where it has reason to believe that an employee may be under the influences of any of these substances or as part of a random test of employees. Each employee is expected to cooperate and consent as a condition of continued employment. Refusal to consent to such testing may result in disciplinary action up to and including termination. We appreciate your help in keeping our club safe and drug-free.

DRUG FREE WORKPLACE ACKNOWLEDGEMENT AND CONSENT FORM

I acknowledge that I have received and read Single Barrel Consulting's Drug Free Workplace Policy and agree to abide by it.

I understand that neither the Drug Free Workplace Policy nor my agreement to abide by its terms create any type of employment contract or contractual obligation on the behalf of Single Barrel Consulting, LLC.

____

Print Name   Signature

SOLICITATION POLICY

Any spoken or written offer of sexual service, by you or a guest, in or outside of the club constitutes solicitation and is strictly against the law. You must never ask a guest to buy a drink or food for you. You must never contract for private parties of any kind. Any guest found soliciting our employees will be asked to leave. Any employee found soliciting a guest will be terminated. You are not allowed to leave with any guest for any reason. Dating any guest is STRICTLY AGAINST COMPANY POLICY.

____

Print Name   Signature

FRATERNIZATION POLICY

Dating guests of the club is forbidden. I, ___________________________________, acknowledge that it is absolutely against the policy of Single Barrel Consulting, LLC for any employee or Lessee of the club to date or socialize in any manner outside the premises with any customer of Single Barrel Consulting, LLC. Furthermore, I promise to follow this policy.

____

Print Name   Signature

SMOKING ENVIRONMENT ACKNOWLEDGMENT

I, ___________________________________ acknowledge that Single Barrel Consulting, LLC is a smoking environment. I further acknowledge that exposure to tobacco smoke may be harmful to my health. By voluntarily choosing to work in a smoking environment, I assume the risk of harm that may come from exposure to environmental smoke and hold harmless Single Barrel Consulting, LLC which has offered me said employment. This acknowledgment in no way modifies my status as an at-will employee.

____

Print Name   Signature

GO HOME TICKET POLICY

All staff members are subject to disciplinary actions. The extent of that action may range from a verbal warning to suspension of two weeks or more. The action will be decided on a case-by-case basis. A preponderance of minor infractions may lead to major discipline. The purpose of this policy is to reduce the amount of confusion and limit the time needed to document common incidences that occur while the club is busy.

The Ticket

The issuance of the "ticket" below is to inform the employee and the HR department of an infraction. The employee will be given the phone number of HR so he/she may text or call to discuss the issue if desired. The manager is expected to text or call HR to explain any details not included on the "Ticket".

Go Home

If the infraction is simple, the manager may choose to send the employee home for the shift. If the employee signs the ticket, he/she may return to work on their next scheduled shift. Refusing to sign the "ticket" defaults to meeting with HR before returning to work. Rather than terminating or firing "on the spot" a default to meeting with HR will give all parties time to reflect and "cool down" before major action is taken.

Meeting with HR

- HR Meetings will be held Mondays through Thursday from 2:00 PM until 4:00 PM. In some cases HR will meet with staff on Fridays from 2:00 PM until 4:00 PM. Friday meetings must be scheduled.
- There will be a consultation with the employee alone and then with the manager involved alone.
- The final meeting will involve both manager and employee. At this time, further action will be determined if needed.

SAMPLE: GO HOME TICKET

Name ____

Date /Date ___________________________________

Performance   <u>0</u>   Attitude   <u>0</u>

Attendance   <u>0</u>   Intoxication   <u>0</u>

GO HOME THIS SHIFT

Emp. Sign Here ________________________________

- OR –

See HR on Monday - Thursday between 2PM and 4PM

____

Manager

By signing this form, I understand that failure to meet with HR after a ticketed incidence requiring a meeting may result in job forfeiture.

____

Employee PRINT NAME

____

Employee Signature

____

Department

EMPLOYMENT ARBITRATION AGREEMENT

In consideration of <u>Single Barrel Consulting, LLC</u> employing me and the mutual promises set forth herein, <u>Single Barrel Consulting, LLC</u> and I, together with our representatives, successors, and assigns hereby agree as follows:

Section I   VOLUNTARY AT-WILL EMPLOYMENT

Unless an employee has a written employment agreement with <u>Single Barrel Consulting, LLC</u>, which provides differently, all employment at <u>Single Barrel Consulting, LLC</u> is "at-will."

That means that employees may be terminated from employment with <u>Single Barrel Consulting, LLC</u> with or without cause, and employees are free to leave the employment of <u>Single Barrel Consulting, LLC</u> with or without cause. Any representation by any <u>Single Barrel Consulting, LLC</u>'s officer or employee contrary to this policy is not binding upon <u>Single Barrel Consulting, LLC</u> unless it is in writing and is signed by the Executive Director with the approval of the Board of Directors.

Section II   ARBITRATION OF DISPUTES

Because of the delay and expense involved in litigation before the state and federal courts, or before the state or federal agencies, <u>Single Barrel Consulting, LLC</u> and I, ____________________________ understand and agree that any claim or dispute arising out of or relating to my recruitment, hiring, employment or termination from employment with <u>Single Barrel Consulting, LLC</u> shall be subject to final and binding arbitration, pursuant to the Federal Arbitration Act 9,U.S.C -1 et seq. and the Colorado Arbitration Act. The arbitration will be conducted in Denver, Colorado.

Claims which must be arbitrated under this agreement include but are not limited to:
- any and all claims on common law, whether in tort or contract;
- any employment discrimination, harassment, or retaliation claims based on federal or state law, including claims based upon Title VII, The Americans with Disabilities Act, and The Age Discrimination in Employment Act;
- claims for violation of the Family Medical Leave Act;
- claims for violation of the Fair Labor Standards Act;
- claims for violation of public policy or for whistleblowing;
- any claim based on any state or federal statute;
- any claim based on any state or federal constitutional provision; and
- any amendments or modifications to such laws.

However, any claim by the Employee for unemployment or workers' compensation benefits is not subject to mandatory arbitration under this agreement.

My agreement to arbitrate any claim or dispute arising out of or relating to my recruitment, , hiring, employment or termination from employment with <u>Single Barrel Consulting, LLC</u> shall include any and all claims brought against any agent, insurer, co-employee, supervisor, manager, office, owner, director, or shareholder of <u>Single Barrel Consulting, LLC</u> present, future or former, if said claim or dispute relates to or arises out of or relating to my recruitment, hiring, employment or termination from employment with <u>Single Barrel Consulting, LLC</u>. Consolidation of separate arbitration proceedings is prohibited.

Arbitration may be initiated by either party providing the other party with a written notice of claim which describes the nature of the dispute and a demand for arbitration. This notice must be given by certified or registered mail, return receipt requested and obtained, or by service authorized for commencement of a civil action.

The arbitration of any dispute under this Agreement shall be conducted pursuant to the then existing arbitration rules and procedure of Dispute Prevention and Resolution, Inc. (DPR) The Parties agree to use the Arbitrator selection procedures set forth by the DPR.
This Agreement regarding arbitration of disputes between myself and <u>Single Barrel Consulting, LLC</u> may only be modified by a writing that is signed by both me and the Executive Director of <u>Single Barrel Consulting, LLC</u>.

<u>Single Barrel Consulting, LLC</u> will pay reasonable costs of arbitration including filing fees and arbitrator expenses. Each party shall his/her/its own attorney's fees and costs, if any. However, the arbitrator may, at his/her discretion, permit the prevailing party to recover fees and costs to the extent permitted by applicable law. Neither party, however, forgoes and substantive rights or remedies as provided by law.

Section III ENTIRE AGREEMENT

I acknowledge and agree that this Agreement contains the entire agreement and understanding between myself and <u>Single Barrel Consulting, LLC</u>. This agreement supersedes all other agreements, whether oral or in writing, relating to the subject matter herein.

Section IV SEVERABILITY OF PROVISION

The parties intend that this agreement be enforceable to the fullest extent permitted by law. Should any term or provision of this Agreement be determined to be illegal, void, or invalid, such terms shall be considered severed or modified to conform to the law, and the remaining terms and provisions of this agreement shall continue in full force and effect

Section V   MISCELLANEOUS

This agreement shall be binding and pass to the benefit of the successors and assigns of <u>Single Barrel Consulting, LLC</u>. This Agreement survives and extends beyond my termination of employment. Waiver by the company of any particular breach of this Agreement by me shall not be deemed a waiver by <u>Single Barrel Consulting, LLC</u> of any of my promises or obligations herein, or of any subsequent breach by me.

I AGREE TO KEEP ALL PROCEEDINGS AND MATTERS SUBJECT TO THIS AGREEMENT COMPLETELY CONFIDENTIAL. HOWEVER, I UNDERSTAND THAT I HAVE THE RIGHT TO RETAIN COUNSEL OF MY CHOICE IF DESIRED.

I UNDERSTAND THAT BY SIGNING THIS AGREEMENT, I RELINQUISH THE RIGHT TO A TRIAL BY A JUDGE, JURY, OR ADMINISTRATIVE AGENCY, OF ANY CLAIM OR DISPUTE RELATING TO OR ARISING OUT OF MY RECRUITMENT, HIRING, EMPLOYMENT OR TERMINATION WITH <u>SINGLE BARREL CONSULTING, LLC</u>.

AGREED AND ACCEPTED

_______________________________   _______________________________
Print Employee Name   Employee Signature

_______________________________   _______________________________
Print Company Rep Name   Company Rep Signature

____
Date

NON-DISCLOSURE OF CONFIDENTIAL INFORMATION

Any information you learn about <u>Single Barrel Consulting, LLC</u> guests, employees or vendors, as a result of working for <u>Single Barrel Consulting, LLC</u> that is not otherwise publicly available constitutes confidential information. The protection of privileged and confidential information, including trade secrets, is vital to the interests and the success of <u>Single Barrel Consulting, LLC</u>. The disclosure, distribution, electronic transmission or copying of Company confidential information is prohibited. Such information includes, but is not limited to compensation data, program and financial information, including information related to donors, and pending projects and proposals. You may not disclose confidential information to anyone who is or is not employed by <u>Single Barrel Consulting, LLC</u> or to other persons employed by <u>Single Barrel Consulting, LLC</u> who do not need to know such information to assist in rendering services. Discussions involving sensitive information should always be held in confidential settings to safeguard the confidentiality of the information. Conversations regarding confidential information generally should not be conducted on cellular phones, or in elevators, restrooms, restaurants, or other places where conversations might be overheard.

_______________________________   _______________________________
Print Name   Signature

CONCLUSION

I understand that the preceding policies are outlined in the <u>Single Barrel Consulting, LLC</u> Policy Manual and that it is my responsibility to know and understand all company policies. By accepting employment with <u>Single Barrel Consulting, LLC</u> I am agreeing to adhere to all policies whether a signature has been obtained or not.

_______________________________   _______________________________
Print Name   Signature

____
Date

Waitress Training Manual

This is a sample training manual. Each department would have specifics designed for their job, but the bulk of the manual will be the same for every employee. Each club will have specifics for state laws and procedures as well. This is a guideline of what should be included in your training manuals.

Contents

INTRODUCTION

It is our goal at Shotgun Willies to create the finest in adult entertainment on the planet. We do this by treating every person who comes through our doors, calls on our phone, or works with us as a special individual. We recognize this "spark" of individuality in ourselves as well as in others and communicate this in an honest and sincere manner.

FIVE STAR SERVICE

At Shotgun Willies we strive for professionalism and teamwork. To reach our goal we follow these guidelines. Keep in mind that not any one point is more important than another; it is the combination that produces Five Star Service.

ATTITUDE AND APPEARANCE - Attitude and appearance go hand-in-hand. If you look good, you feel good and if you feel good, you look good. If you act like you're having fun, those around you will have fun. There is no room on the set for personal problems. Not only does it affect your performance, it affects those around you. Our guests come here to see beautiful women. They notice small things like hair and fingernails. We understand that it is difficult to be "perfect" every day, but we expect you to do the very best you can.

KNOWLEDGE - Know your duties and responsibilities thoroughly. Know procedures and promotions. If there is something you don't know or understand, ASK. The worst thing you can say to a guest is, "I don't know". I don't know suggests you don't care, it is far better to say, "I'll find out," or "I'll check on that for you."

SERVICE - We cannot stress the "importance of smiling" enough. One smile will do what a thousand words cannot. We cater to our guests. We do the extra little things to make them feel special. "Every Guest is Entitled to the Same Service."

BUILD A CLIENTELE - A regular clientele will increase your tips. Learn the art of small talk. Learn to be witty without being catty. Make sure every guest feels welcome and special. We refer to our audience as our "guest" rather than "customer" – we expect them to be treated as such. Learn the names of the guests and make sure they know yours. They will ask for you the next time they come in.

APPRECIATION - It is because of our audience that we have a SHOW. Without them, we would have NO SHOW. This includes the guest who cannot afford a large tip as well as the guest who can. Always thank a guest for a tip no matter what the amount. Let them know you are glad they are here. When they leave, thank them for coming and invite them back.

JOB DESCRIPTION

The breadth of this text is testimony to the fact that there is a substantial amount of knowledge necessary to successfully perform as a professional Waitress. Yet, no guide on commercial Waitressing would be complete without a thorough discussion on the refined, diplomatic art of guest relations.

While nearly every guest, manager, or club owner will have a different notion on what the Waitress job descriptions are, the following is an attempt to provide the generally accepted parameters of the position.

A Professional Waitress must:
- Remain vigilant against selling alcohol to minors.
- Continually strive to improve his or her artistic and technical expertise.
- Honor and oblige when intervention is in the public's best interest.
- Handle all monetary transactions in an honest and forthright manner.
- Place composure before his or her emotions.
- Oversee a legally complying bar.
- Remain sober and alert when representing the employer.
- Work expediently and accept responsibility for his or her actions.
- Maintain a clean and health-conscious work area.
- Provide exemplary service and hospitality.

First and foremost, Shotgun Willies is an Entertainment Club. As an employee, you are an essential part of the show we provide. This script will explore numerous fine points regarding the highly skilled art of providing our audience with professional beverage service. This section also contains material delineating what the managers and owners of Shotgun Willie's Show Club expect of their Waitresses as performers in our show.

EMPLOYEE DRESS CODE

Waitresses are part of the show, and as a full cast member, we expect you to be professionally dressed in quality eveningwear. This includes a red evening dress or gown with red or black high heels. Hair should be neatly trimmed and styled. Nails should be clean and in good repair.

GUEST INTERACTION

A Waitress should make a concerted effort to avoid listening in on guests' conversations, unless he/she is addressed directly, and avoid engaging guests in extended unnecessary conversation. He/she should remain, at all times, polite and courteous, and friendly with the guests.

By any means possible, Waitresses should avoid becoming embroiled in inflammatory conversations. Discussions about politics and religion can often become quite heated. It is therefore far safer to gradually withdraw from the conversation. As a Waitress, taking sides exacts a heavy toll on tips.

To become a better conversationalist, a Waitress should read the daily newspaper in an effort to stay abreast of current events and happenings in sports.

DIFFICULT OR UNRULY GUESTS

There may be occasions when the ingestion of alcohol may cause a guest to become unruly or belligerent. If you feel you are ever in danger or in a situation beyond your control, remove yourself from the situation and immediately notify your Manager.

ALCOHOL AWARENESS

Shotgun Willie's strictly adheres to the liquor laws of this state. It is your job as bar personnel to strictly enforce these laws and our company policies in order to keep our liquor licenses.

As a leader in the industry, we respond to the need for intelligence and responsibility regarding the consumption of alcohol. The manager will take all necessary steps to educate the staff about alcohol awareness and the applicable laws.

Below are some of the major laws that are used nationwide. All bar personnel are required to maintain current TIPS certification or comparable alcohol awareness training.

SUMMARY OF POLICIES AND LAWS
You must adhere to the following policies:

- Do not knowingly allow an intoxicated person into the club. Please notify the manager if an intoxicated person does enter.
- Do not knowingly allow an intoxicated person to leave our club with the intention of driving.
- Offer cab service or other means of travel to prevent an intoxicated guest from driving.
- Offer complimentary coffee or soft drinks to intoxicated persons in order that time will help to sober them.
- We do not "back up" more than 2 drinks.

Your cooperation is needed to maintain an atmosphere of responsible drinking. Please notify a manager of any intoxicated persons and take the time to make sure that all your co-workers are aware of the situation. Your primary responsibility is for the safety and well-being of the guest. Equally important is your own protection, as the law holds you responsible if you do not adhere to the laws listed below:

- All entertainer must present a Drink Ticket for every alcoholic drink they consume. They must also be wearing the official wristband denoting that they are of age to drink and not currently on the "No Drink List".
- It is against the law to:
  - Serve alcohol after 4:00 AM or before 7:00 AM. Note: All glasses must be taken up before 4:00 AM.

- Serve a known alcoholic at any time.
- Serve a disorderly person.
- Serve an intoxicated person; anyone who exhibits the following signs of intoxication:
    - A change in personality
    - Slurred speech
    - Loss of coordination
    - Irrational statements
    - Unable to focus or glassy/bloodshot eyes

- Serve any person under the age of 21 or any person who does not have/show one of the following forms of identification:
    - Valid state driver's license with photo
    - Valid state identification card with photo
    - Current military identification card with photo
    - Current alien registration card with photo
    - Valid passport with photo

FOOD SERVICE

Food must be served hot and fresh. Bad food service will ruin a tip quicker than poor drink service. Learn to count the songs playing to insure you retrieve your food in a timely manner. Most songs are about 4 minutes long.

Pick-up Times
Appetizers: 5-6 mins, 8 max (1 to 2 songs)
Entrees: 10-12 mins, max (2 to 3 songs)
Steak: (well) 15 mins, max (3 to 4 songs)

YOUR SECTION

Teamwork and professional courtesy are of utmost importance.
- There is no "I" in T-E-A-M.
- Fighting over guests will not be tolerated.
- If you need help, ask for it. If someone needs help, offer it.
- NEVER walk past empty bottles or glasses
- ALWAYS acknowledge an incoming guest.
- If you have opened a tab with a guest who wishes to move to another section, you MUST transfer the tab to the waitress/bartender in that section.
- NEVER ask a guest to close a tab.

When working with more than one waitress, the manager will communicate as to which section of the club you are to service and which well you are to use. Always be aware of entire room as to cover everyone. If a guest sits in another waitress' section, you may greet the guest and take the order but you must turn it over to the waitress in that area.

Guests of the club DO NOT belong to any staff member or entertainer. We encourage you to invite friends to the club but be aware, if they sit in another section, that waitress is obligated to wait on your friends

SERVICE WELL

The service well/waitress station is not a social area. Be courteous to your co-workers and do not stand around the well and talk. Leaving a tray in the service well while you are away is rude and makes it difficult for other waitresses to use the well.
Do not eat or smoke in this area by order of the Health Department. If you are drinking a beverage, always use a straw.

TICKETS

COMP TICKET (Complementary Drinks)

When a guest gives you a card for a complimentary drink, be sure to check for the manager's or owner's signature. Comp Tickets are only valid for drinks $9.00 and under. If possible, find out the reason for the comp. (Birthday, Trivia, VIP, Participation, etc.) This will help your tips. Get involved with your guests.
Complimentary drinks are to be rung in the POS system under a "Comp" tab. At the end of the night, your comp tickets should match the amount of drinks rang into this tab. At the end the evening, the manager will close out the tab for you and you will turn in your comp tickets with your checkout.

SPILL TICKET

Waitresses should be well acquainted with the beverage operations' spill rules. In most cases we do not replace spilled drinks. If an entertainer should spill a guest's drink, she will be asked to replace it. The reasons or the spill are as follows: you ordered the wrong drink, drink is unacceptable to the guest, you cannot find guest who ordered the drink, etc. At the end of the evening the Manager will ask you to explain spilled drinks and will close them out.

VOID TICKET

Voids consist of any drink or food that was NOT prepared but incorrectly punched in to the POS system such as mistakes or 86'd items.

CREDIT CARD TICKET

WE DO NOT RUN CASH TABS. Any Waitress that chooses to run a Cash Tab is subject to termination and will be responsible for payment of said Cash Tab should the guest walk out. If a guest would like to run a Credit Card Tab with you, please follow these guidelines. We accept VISA, MasterCard, Discover and American Express.

Ask for the guest's credit card and matching valid identification. Do not accept a card that has expired, or a card that says Jane Doe when the guest is John Doe. We do not accept credit card type gift cards.

EXAMPLE
- ALWAYS explain to our guest that the billing name will be Bavaria Inn Restaurant.
- We only accept cards with a chip. If the chip doesn't read, they must come up with another form of payment.
- Get driver's license & credit card and make sure they match.
- Pay close attention to all credit cards. If a card reaches its maximum it will decline and you will have to ask for another form of payment. DO NOT bring the customer anything else if card has been declined.
- Write down type of ID, state, and number on form as proof of verification.
- If the guest is only paying for that round. Give credit card and ID back to customer.
- If the guests would like to keep the tab open, have the guest sign the authorization form and return the card and ID at the close of the tab.
- Give the imprint, the Aloha printout, and the signed CC slip to the bartender to close. Make sure the CC slip is on top.

NOTE: WE DO NOT ACCEPT GIFT CARDS OR ANY PREPAID CREDIT CARDS THAT DO NOT HAVE A CHIP AND A NAME THAT MATCHES THE GUEST'S ID

DREAM GIRL DOLLARS (DGD)
Dream Girl Dollars are house money. Guests can buy them with a credit card as an alternative to getting cash from the ATM. This is an open and close transaction.

- We DO NOT run tabs for Dream Girl Dollars. Only bring the amount the guest asks for and not an amount requested by an entertainer.
- Guest must sign the "chit" (the piece of paper that has the amount of dream girl dollars) every time they order Dream Girl Dollars. This verifies that the customer wants the amount of Dream Girl Dollars that they just received.
- If the ordered DGD amount is greater than $100 then you must get a Manager signature as well.
- There is a 15% surcharge on DGD purchases. Example: guest orders $100 in DGD's. Their credit card will be charged $115.
- DGD's are good for table dances, to tip the entertainers or support staff, and to pay for food and drinks.
- If a guest uses DGDs to pay for drinks you can trade them into the bartender same as cash. Let a manager know if customer is using DGDs for drinks.
- If a customer tips you with DGDs you must trade them in with the cashier at the end of your shift.

OPENING YOUR SHIFT

If you are opening the club in the morning, you will need to set out ashtrays and condiments. Check the linens on the tables and the tabletops to see that they are presentable. Change or wipe as needed. Straighten chairs and check that they are clean and in good repair. If you find a table or chair that in in need of service., flag it and tell the Manager on Duty.

Check the flyers and advertisements to see that they are current and in good repair. If you find a flyer out of date, please pull it, and replace with current information.

Wipe down all food and liquor menus. Replace any that are damaged or out of date. Make coffee and tea for the day.
Greet the guests at the door as they come in!

ENDING YOUR SHIFT

If you are working a day or mid shift, make sure your section is clean before turning it over to the next waitress. Introduce the new waitress to ALL your guests. (This gives them a chance to tip you before you leave.) Transfer tabs as needed to the waitress following you. If you have served the guest and he does not chose to tip you before you leave, print a copy of the tab and give it to the new waitress so she will know what share of the tip belongs to you. She should leave your share of the tip in an envelope in the safe.

Check the kitchen for clean silverware and roll what is available. Check the napkin and condiments and stock as needed.

If you are working until close, you will be responsible for Last Call and final clean up. Last Call is usually given at 1:30 am and lasts about three songs. This is your time to be sure each of your guests knows Last Call has been announced. Ask your guests if they wish to continue to add anything to their tab before closing.

When the last song of the night is announced, all Waitresses should have closed all Credit Card tickets. Waitresses may have only one cash ticket open at this time, as their tabs should have been closed during Last Call.

DO NOT PICK UP ASHTRAYS UNTIL AFTER THE BUILDING IS CLEARED!
We don't want guests putting out cigarettes on clean tables or the floor.

Everyone should help floor staff remove all drinks from guests and clear the floor. Also, help gather glassware throughout the club and return to the bar.

Please refer to Cleanup Responsibility Sheet if you are unclear as to specific clean up duties.

GENERAL RULES AND INFORMATION

ATTENDANCE & TARDINESS

Excessive absences or tardiness will not be tolerated and may be cause for suspension or termination. Customary discipline procedures as follows:

- Depending on the infraction, discipline is at the Manager's discretion and will be a verbal warning, write-up, suspension, or termination.
- Work schedules are made up each week to suit the needs of the show.
  - Should there be a conflict with your personal needs, please make your manager aware by writing your request in advance.
  - A schedule request should be in writing and given to the scheduling manager one to two weeks in advance.
  - Whenever possible we will try to accommodate you, but remember, the show must come first.
- Schedules are posted on the bulletin board each week.
  - If there are two weeks posted, the second week is tentative.
  - Changes or trades in current week must have a manager's written consent and be initialed.
  - You are responsible for knowing your weekly schedule.
- Once the schedule is made and posted, we expect you to be on time.
  - You are expected to be in Costume and prepared to perform at your scheduled time.
  - A tardy is not being on the set within 5 minutes of your scheduled time.
  - If for any reason you are going to be late or miss your shift, please extend us the courtesy of a phone call.
    - Please call and speak to a MANAGER 2 to 3 hours before your shift is scheduled to begin.

PAY PERIODS

- Employees are paid biweekly.
- Checks will be in the manager's office after 3PM on the Friday following the end of the pay period.

BREAKS

- Please do not leave the floor without notifying a manager.
- You will have to take your break when the manager has time to cover the booth.
- You will be allowed to take a break before 9PM at which time you may retrieve cigarettes or other personal items for using during your break.
- Meals will be eaten in the employee break area.
- Cigarette smoking is allowed in designated areas only.
- Please be courteous to those who do not smoke and keep this area clean. Wash your hands often and do not chew gum.

PHONE AND PERSONAL ITEMS

A personal item is any item not considered a part of your uniform. This includes cell phones, food, gum, energy drinks, coffee, cigarettes, purses, wallets, etc. Please keep all personal items in your locker.

BULLETIN BOARD

There are bulletin boards for general information pertaining to all employees, such as health notices, lost and found, etc. You will find your weekly schedule posted on the Casting Board, usually located next to the general information board.

CURRENT PROMOTIONS

Please keep our guests informed of all upcoming promotions, either through the use of flyers, DJ announcements and/or telling each guest personally. Occasionally, you will be asked to wear corresponding costumes for a promotion. You are to supply your own costumes for these events.

CONFIDENTIALITY OF CLUB INFORMATION

It is the responsibility of all employees to safeguard sensitive information. The nature of our business, and the economic well-being of Shotgun Willies, is dependent upon protecting and maintaining proprietary information. Your continued role with us is contingent upon compliance with this policy. Please note that this also includes Social Media as it pertains to always promoting us in a positive light. Any negative remarks or posts about Shotgun Willies, or any of its employees can result in disciplinary action.

DRESSING ROOM

This is your private area away from crowds and noise. Keep this area clean and conduct yourself in a friendly manner with the other employees. Respect the space, property and personal lives of others. Lockers are provided for valuables and personal property. You must provide your own lock and are responsible for the privacy of the combination. Print your name and the date on a piece of tape, supplied by the manager, and place it on the locker. Shotgun Willies is not responsible for lost or stolen items. Management reserves the right to search all lockers and their contents at any time.

EVALUATIONS

To maintain proper standards an evaluation sheet will be used as a tool by your Manager to discover hidden talents as well as areas of improvement. All evaluations will be confidential. Employees may be evaluated each month. A meeting will be set up with your casting director to discuss your scores. Should you fail any area of an evaluation, you will be given a specified amount of time in which to improve. Failure to improve may result in termination. You will find an example of the evaluation sheet and explanation of grading at the back of these guidelines.

SPOUSES AND/OR SIGNIFICANT OTHERS

It is Shotgun Willies policy that significant others stay off the set while you are working. If they are picking you up, they may arrive 15 minutes before you are scheduled to end your performance. Please notify your manager when they arrive. Special exceptions with prior notification: your significant other may be allowed in for bachelor or office parties. You may also come in with your significant other on your day off with Management approval.

SOLICITATION

Any spoken or written offer of sexual service, by you or the guest, in or out of the club constitutes solicitation and is against the law. You may never ask a guest to buy a drink or food for you. You must never contract for private parties of any kind. You must never direct a guest to ask another cast member. Any guest found soliciting our employees or our contractors shall be asked to leave. Any employee or contractor found soliciting a guest will be terminated. You are not allowed to leave with any guest for any reason. Dating our guest or other staff members is STRICTLY FORBIDDEN.

STEALING/THEFT

Any theft is considered serious and may result in termination. The Management views the following as theft. This list is not all-inclusive:

- Taking personal property from a guest or co-worker.
- Not turning in lost articles to the office.
- Taking any equipment, i.e., glasses, ashtrays, towels, etc.
- Giving away unauthorized drinks or food to guest or co-worker.
- Taking unauthorized drinks or food.
- Taking change from a table or bar before a guest has acknowledged it as a tip.
- Taking tips from co-workers or withholding money from tip pools.
- Deliberate overcharging, undercharging, or shortchanging.
- Not ringing up admissions, food, or drinks.

TIPPING

Henceforth, to comply with the Fair Labor Standards Act:

SHOTGUN WILLIES HAS A POLICY OF NO MANDATORY TIP OUT BY ANY EMPLOYEE OR STAFF MEMBER FROM ANY OTHER EMPLOYEE OR STAFF MEMBER WITH THE EXCEPTION OF A WAITRESS TO A BARTENDER AND/OR COOK AND A BARTENDER TO A BAR-BACK AND/OR COOK.

The standard tip for your bartender is 10% of your total tips and 5% to the cook.

APPENDIX

WAITRESS EVALUATION FORM

SHOTGUN WILLIES

WAITRESS EVALUATION FORM

WAITRESS ______________________________ **DATE** ________

SUPERVISOR ______________________________ Comments

DRINK SALES Sales per hour as compared to others.	0	1	2	3	4	5 ______________
DEPENDABILITY Ability to follow a schedule. Attendace.	0	1	2	3	4	5 ______________
COMPATABILITY Respect for others. Team player.	0	1	2	3	4	5 ______________
COOPERATION Willingness to help others and management.	0	1	2	3	4	5 ______________
KNOWLEDGE Job related education, skills, and experience.	0	1	2	3	4	5 ______________
APPEARANCE Personal habits, grooming, and uniform	0	1	2	3	4	5 ______________
TABLE SERVICE Upselling, guest interaction, service.	0	1	2	3	4	5 ______________
CLEANLINESS Appearance of tables, ashtrays, glasses, chairs, section.	0	1	2	3	4	5 ______________
ACCURACY Absence of errors/spills	0	1	2	3	4	5 ______________
INITATIVE Volunteers for extra duties and charities.	0	1	2	3	4	5 ______________

Total Score ________

WAITRESS SIDE WORK – CLOSING SHIFT

Date: _________________ Manager Sig: _________________________________

Waitress/s ____

____

MANAGERS MUST CHECK THESE DUTIES EACH DAY
BEFORE YOU LEAVE THE FLOOR!

- ☐ Clean waitress station computers, printers, and service area. Remove all personal items.
- ☐ Stock waitress wells – straws, napkins, rollups, staples, credit card carbons, printer tape.
- ☐ Clean and stock bottle service station – mixer decanters, glassware, white napkins, silver cups with red & black straws neatly with cocktail napkins inside.
- ☐ Dump and wipe out all ice buckets, store in bottom of cupboard.
- ☐ Clean soda gun; wipe the hose.
- ☐ Wash and roll all silverware. Stock each station with roll-ups.
- ☐ Gather *ALL* ashtrays, (tables, DJ booth, restroom, etc.). Clean and store in bottle service area.
- ☐ Clean all cigar ashtrays and return to front door station.
- ☐ Wipe all glass tops, both sides with Windex and dry paper towels.
- ☐ Replace linen if needed.
- ☐ Wipe down kitchen doors and the walls around trash containers.
- ☐ Wipe down all flat wood surfaces, including railings.
- ☐ Wipe down the front of all cabinets and shelves.
- ☐ Wipe down all menus and replace in holders.
- ☐ Place CLEAN condiments in the cooler. Marry if low.
- ☐ Stock and organize barrel room with bottle service items, make it tidy to the eye.

9 781942 665144